Warehouse Life

Your Guide To Unconventional Living Spaces

Discover how to live in lofts, warehouses and commercial spaces at a fraction of what you are paying for an apartment or house.

Michael Villa

Disclaimer

I am not a lawyer or real estate broker or accountant and this is probably all bad advice. I take no responsibility for any action you choose to take based on anything in this book. My situation may be different from yours and laws or regulations in your area may be different or may change since this was written. I live in a warehouse! Why would you take advice from me anyway? All content in this book is for informational purposes only. I am not suggesting or advocating any activity whatsoever. I do not recommend, endorse, or suggest that anyone take any action that is not legal in your area.

ISBN13: 978-1-943257-00-3

Those who are slaves to their own beliefs
will never find freedom.

Warehouse Life Blog

More resources and information are available at
www.WarehouseLife.com

What would you do with more space?

Introduction – What are Unconventional Living Spaces?

Discover how you can:

- **Save money**

- **Live in an unusual and exciting space**

- **Have enough room to work on projects**

- **Avoid neighbors**

- **Enjoy solitude**.

Does saving money and having more space sound appealing?

I remember when I was young and watched a TV show called Vega$ (1978-1981) starring Robert Urich where he lived in a commercial space with a garage door that opened and let him pull his car practically into the living room. What could be any cooler? I dreamed of having such a place to live. As I got older, social programming changed my perception and I, as most people, became programmed with the limiting idea that we should live in a house or an apartment and it must have a bedroom and a kitchen and a shower, otherwise it is not livable. My dream was set aside for what I thought were practical reasons. Fortunately, I eventually broke out of this programming and found a place I am happier with than any house or apartment I ever lived in before.

My only regret is that I did not do this years earlier.

What is an unconventional living space?

The term unconventional living space often brings up images of people living in missile silos in the Nevada desert or in apocalypse-proof underground bunkers. Though these are unconventional, they are not the only types of unconventional living spaces.

Other types of unconventional living spaces include warehouses, retail sales space, trailers, shipping containers, remote commercial service buildings that are no longer used, government buildings where the agency moved to another building, churches or unused schools. Many of these are hard to rent or sell due to the work required to make them usable for a business. That makes them perfect for live-work space.

Movies and TV programs show unconventional living spaces.

- *Vega$ (1978-1981)*
- *Tron Legacy* 2010 has the protagonist in a shipping container
- In *Enemy of the State* 1998 there is a warehouse
- *The Conversation* 1974 has characters living in a warehouse
- *Wanted: Dead or Alive* 1986
- *Winters Tale* 2014
- *Karam*
- The French romantic thriller *Diva*
- *Unmade Beds*
- *Nash* TV show
- *Blind Beast* 1969
- *Cavemen* 2013

I am not interested in "roughing it" myself. I like comfort and I will reveal how you can find a location that meets your needs and how to make it not only as comfortable as a house, but in some cases more comfortable, at a lower cost!

A residential area is an area zoned and primarily used for personal housing. A commercial or industrial area is an area zoned and primarily used for certain types of businesses. There are good reasons for zoning these separately. No one wants to live next to a loud manufacturing business, and businesses want to be in an area that is kept clean and is convenient for their clients to visit. Having a bunch of families with children leaving toys around or taking up parking spaces or being the lone business in an area that otherwise might draw customers from surrounding businesses is not what most businesses want. It is usually prohibited for someone to live in a commercial area, but there are ways around this which I will cover in more detail shortly.

Commercial rent can be much less than residential rent. This comes from a number of factors including lower taxes and less desirable locations compared to residential areas.

There is an entire subculture living in

unconventional spaces.

Let's talk space.

Houses are designed in a very inefficient manner. They have walls where they are not needed and no walls where they are needed. You cannot adjust rooms to meet your needs either. I had a house with a fairly large square footage of 1700sqft. One small bedroom was used for storage, but that meant boxes were stacked around the walls and the walking path in the center was completely wasted, plus I could only stack things so high due to the seven foot ceiling

height. I also had a nice big bedroom, but what good does it do me when the living room is too small? I can't move that extra bedroom space to the living area when I need it or to the garage when I want to work on a project, so the large bedroom space was wasted all of the time except for the short part of the day when I was getting up or going to bed. I didn't need the space when I was sleeping.

In this house, I had a patio that I rarely used, and an odd-shaped kitchen that meant some of it was never used efficiently, so more wasted floor space. It was very inefficient and I never had enough room to work on my art and sculpting projects. The kitchen island was constantly covered with a project, and the cramped garage where I had a makeshift shop had a small table covered with other art projects I was working on. I was constantly shifting things around and never had enough storage or work space.

A large space is the benefit of a warehouse. You have some fixed rooms for basic living and a huge space you can arrange any way you want. If you are an artist or work on big projects then you know how valuable space can be.

Today the separation between work and home is not so clear. In the 1950's you left home at 7 AM and returned at 6 PM. Your work was left behind and you enjoyed home life.

Today, we are tweeting on our phone when we are riding in elevators, checking email for client questions during TV commercials, awake in bed at 2 am while the kids are sleeping, and answering emails from the boss on a laptop. Why is sleeping in your office prohibited, but *officing* where you sleep is not? If your neighbor can run a business from his home fixing computers or knitting sweaters, as long as he is not disturbing the neighbors, then why should you not be able to run a home from your business in a commercial location if you are not causing a disruption? I say you should!

Let's talk cost.

At one time I was renting an office and a house. I rented a commercial space for my computer programming business and lived in a 900 square foot house. When my business was expanding, I first rented the space thinking I might have no choice but to give up my house and live in the office if the business did not do well, but it did well enough that I could cover the bills. This meant that I was paying rent on a large office and on a small house. What a waste!

I found that I spent little time at the office. I would do what work I had to do, then go home as soon as I could because I had a computer at home in one of the bedrooms where I could work in comfort. I could take a break and watch TV, cook something to eat, work on an art project for a while and even take a nap. I could not do any of that at the office because it was not set up for anything useful other than work.

Eventually business dropped off and I decided I needed to cut costs. I realized it was cheaper to move to a larger 1700 square foot house and run my business out of it instead of renting a small house and a large office. At that point, I was still a slave to my social programming so I did things exactly backwards. The change did save me about $1000 a month, but I soon outgrew the house and the poor layout was a constant issue. I never had enough space. Having a larger house did not solve my problem because I could not use the space I had.

I was living alone in a three-bedroom house and paying $2300/month for a 1700 square foot house. In reality, less than 900 square feet were usable. I looked for a larger house many times, but they were too expensive. I looked for a house with a large storage building many times, but those are almost impossible to find. No one has a 2000 square foot house with a 2000 square foot storage building in the back yard.

Compare Warehouse/Office vs. Residential Costs

LA Warehouse/Office Spaces

- 1600sqft $785/month
- 1300sqft $1215/mo
- 500sqft office with 1200sqft warehouse in downtown LA $1600/month
- 1500sqft $1600/month office warehouse in Glendora CA
- 3000sqft $2900/month with warehouse, office, yard, restroom, parking.

Residential Los Angeles County California

- 1600sqft $2650/mo 3 bedroom townhouse
- 1143sqft $2200/mo 3 bed 2 bath condo
- 950sqft for $1700/mo 2 bedroom
- 820sqft $2047/mo 1 bedroom, not even an ocean view, just a view of the next apartment complex.
- 700sqft $1430/month 1 bedroom
- 600sqft $1550 1 bedroom
- 2850sqft $3496/mo 5 bedroom 4 bath
- 2199 sqft $2800/mo 5 bedroom older house
- 700sqft $1475/mo 1br 1 bath

Atlanta GA Office/Warehouse Space

- 2000sqft $1350/mo office/warehouse.
- 1000sqft warehouse with small office $600/month

Atlanta GA House Rental

- 1225sqft $1460/mo 3 bedroom
- 900sqft $929/mo for 2 bedroom

You can see how much cheaper commercial space is compared to residential rentals.

Check craigslist.org or do a web search to find prices in your area

I then woke-up, broke out of my social programming which had falsely convinced me I had to live in a house or apartment, and realized I could live in a warehouse. I moved to a 2100 square foot industrial space with 16 ft ceilings in the warehouse area and nice separate offices in the front. This space allowed me to store all my stuff on the top level over the offices and I still had the office space to live. The 1500 sq ft warehouse area was available for my projects. The office area was heated and air-conditioned so it was very comfortable. The actual office square footage was smaller than my previous house which meant it cost less to heat and cool too.

My house rent was $2300 per month, plus I had to pay utilities and other expenses. Most of these expenses went away when I moved to a commercial space. My commercial rent included trash, sewer and water. There was no yard to mow and the landlord took care of landscaping.

After I moved, the gas and electric bills both dropped due to heating and cooling a smaller space and having a more efficient AC system.

I had been paying a total of $2767 per month for the house including utilities. After moving to my commercial space which had a $1600 per month base rent, I was paying a total of $1840 including utilities. That is almost a $1000 per month savings and I had more space. It is like having a five-car garage plus a living space.

Here is what I was paying for my 1700sqft house compared to my expenses after moving to a 2100 sqft warehouse:

Monthly House Expenses		Warehouse Expenses
Trash	$27.00	$0
Sewer	$40.00	$0
Water	$25.00	$0
Natural Gas	$50.00	$10.00
Electricity	$220.00	$180.00
Insurance	$50.00	$50.00
Yard Mowing	$55.00	$0
	-------------	---------------
Utilities Total	$467.00	$240.00
Rent	$2,300.00	$1,600.00
	Total Monthly Expenses	
House	$2,767.00	Warehouse: $1,840.00
		=$927.00 Savings

Commercial rent varies widely. Large spaces obviously cost more. It pays to shop around. The area that may not be ideal for many businesses is usually ideal for a live-work space. This means you can often find less expensive commercial spaces in out-of-the-way locations.

How many bathrooms can one or two people use at once? Moving to a larger house gains bedrooms and bathrooms but not real space. If you rented a house like this because you needed space for projects or an art studio, most of it is wasted. You don't need more small rooms or extra bathrooms when you can only use one at a time anyway. Houses are not built for people who need wide open space.

I would rather live in my commercial space than in a 10 million dollar mansion. If I had a mansion, the first thing I would want to do is build an industrial-style storage building to work on projects and then I would spend much of my time in it working on projects. So why not just have a really nice office in the industrial building to sleep and save $10M by not buying the mansion?

Who needs a bunch of rooms that have to be maintained and heated or cooled, or a nice lawn that someone has to mow? The money I save on rent lets me feel free to rent a party space if I want to entertain more than a few friends. So what if it costs $200 to rent a party space for a few hours when I am saving so much each month compared to renting a house?

My 2100 square foot space is actually larger than a similar residential space because I have over 500 square feet of additional storage above my office area.

Living in commercially or industrially zoned areas is not uncommon, but it is also not legal except in special circumstances. I will outline those circumstances and explain how this lifestyle can be accomplished successfully whether or not you get permission.

Is this for you? – Changing how you think about where you live

Living in a warehouse makes you different. Taking a date to your tiny and messy apartment may seem creepy, but taking her to your warehouse loft is an adventure. Being a starving artist in a studio apartment may seem noble, but being a successful artist in a warehouse live-work space is much more comfortable.

Find the space that matches your needs and who you are, not the cookie cutter spaces offered to the generic masses as cramped apartments or poorly designed homes or extravagant homes that are horribly expensive.

Finding a loft space that was commercial and has been rezoned as residential is a dream many people have. Such spaces are usually very expensive if you can find one available at all.

There are people who buy commercial spaces and spend hundreds of thousands of dollars converting them into living spaces. They often buy retail or commercial buildings in residential areas and have the zoning changed. These people buy gas stations or retail corner grocery stores in a residential area because those are easier to have rezoned as residential since they are already in a residential area. The obvious problem here is that you have to buy the property which is expensive and you have to rebuild it which is more expensive. I will not cover that kind of conversion and will focus on rentals because they require less work and are far less expensive. My goal is to show you how you can live in an alternative space and save money, not spend it. This book is about renting commercial space and making it into a livable space.

You may have been scared off the idea of living in a commercial space from watching TV shows about massive conversions of artist lofts or closed schools which seemed out of reach due to the massive construction costs and permit nightmares. Those shows on warehouse conversions are about the hard way to do it and are very expensive because that makes for good TV. There is no reason to go to such expense or trouble. Converting a warehouse/office space to a livable space is easy and less expensive than a one month's rent when done correctly.

In other countries(not the US/Canada) people live in caves or handmade huts. A shipping container can be turned into a home. These people survive very well and often consider their home to be very comfortable. In the US such a home would be considered below the poverty line. These people have a different view. They see their homes as practical and filling their needs.

Multiple generations may live in the same cave or small hut. In Europe many apartments are very small. The people who rent these do not stay in them all day. They spend most of their time away from where they live. They choose a living space that matches their lifestyle, one where they only come home to sleep and spend most of their time outside. There are many alternatives to living the way we have been told we should live.

Consider your situation carefully. Living in a commercial space would not work for someone with children or someone socially active who has lots of people visiting constantly. A spouse may not be as crazy about the lifestyle so it is best suited to the bachelor or bachelorette who enjoys freedom and self-expression without the limits of a regular house. It is also great for artists, photographers, engineers and others who need space to work on projects. Some of us get up late at night to work when we have an idea or an artistic inspiration and want to work on a project right then.

Roommates of similar ilk can split the costs, further reducing expenses. Those who enjoy alone time can find living with no neighbors in a large space liberating. At 6 PM almost everyone goes home and you don't have to listen to music or TV from a drunk neighbor's apartment or slamming doors and cars coming and going all night the way you do in an apartment.

Don't think you are an artist? Become one! Pick any art form you are interested in and BAM! You are an artist!

If you have a history of not paying your rent on time or have had problems with landlords on a regular basis, this may not be for you. To successfully live in a commercial location, you need to keep a low profile and not cause problems.

Pets such as dogs may be acceptable if you have no neighbors, such as if you have an isolated building not connected to others where the animal will not disturb other businesses. Cats make less noise and may be easier to keep. The best pets are ones that make no noise and do not have to be walked. If you must have your pair of Great Danes with you, then a commercial space would have to be chosen that works for that lifestyle.

If you have lots of parties, commercial spaces may not work for you unless you have a remote location with no neighbors, such as a remote farm warehouse. If your business is hosting parties and you have the permits, then you can hold private parties it in your space. I would not recommend having big parties in your commercial space and certainly not on a regular basis. Even if it is after business hours, it will cause you problems with the other tenants and the landlord. If you rent a church or other large space that is designed as a meeting location, then it is not unusual for events to be held there, so having 10 or 20 friends over would not stand out as unusual.

If you are the type of person who needs to be outside a lot and spends lots of time on your patio or in the yard, then you should look for a space that meets your needs. You might look for a golf course that you could run as a golf course to pay the rent or sublet to someone to run as a business. Look for other outdoor oriented commercial spaces or isolated spaces with no neighbors.

This lifestyle is best for someone single. I say that because a single person with one car will more easily find a location where he or she can park that car inside a warehouse area. A couple or a person with a roommate may have difficulty finding a location where they can conveniently park two vehicles inside. This depends on the space you rent, but I am considering that most people will rent a warehouse/office combo space. Such a space usually allows one vehicle to be easily pulled in. Even if the warehouse is big, two cars may be too much unless it is really big. I have a large space but would have to do some shuffling to keep two cars inside or would have to sacrifice a lot of work space unless I was willing to pull the cars out when I wanted to work on a big project.

A combination office/warehouse space is the easiest to convert to a living space because the offices are air conditioned and heated, are already divided into usable rooms, already have a bathroom with plumbing and have a large warehouse area for work projects or art projects. A warehouse/office may not be a good match if you like to go outdoors a lot or need to talk to neighbors a lot. A more remote service building/warehouse in the forest or a retail space next to a park may be a better match. If you live in a warehouse/office space

Stand-alone or corner spaces are the best choices.

and spend a lot of time chatting with neighbors, walking around outside, or they see you coming in but not leaving routinely, then it will eventually become clear that you live there. It is better to keep your distance from neighbors. You can be friendly, but you can be friendly once a month. If your neighbors see you come in and then do not see you for a couple of days they will assume you left when they were busy or did not come in to work that day, and they won't think about it any further. They may see you leave and never see you come back, perhaps because you return after business hours. They will not be suspicious about you leaving. Suspicion comes when they see you come in when everyone else is leaving or leave when everyone else is arriving or if your personal vehicle sits out front all night and is seen by the one or two people who come in at 9 PM to get some late-night work finished.

If you enjoy the solitary lifestyle, if you work at home and may not leave home for two or three days in a row, then this lifestyle may fit your needs very well. If you need to get out more often, then you should look for a location where your behavior will not arouse suspicion or where there are no neighbors.

In Japan, some workers cannot afford to return home after work. They leave work, then are homeless and sit on the streets, sleeping in a suit, leaning against their briefcase. In the morning they go back in their office, wash up and start work again.

You should be handy. If something needs to be fixed, you will fix it yourself or you will hire someone to fix it. You will not be calling the landlord every time the sink is backed up. There are two reasons for this. First, it is going to be your responsibility under a commercial lease to handle minor upkeep. Second, you do not want to bug your landlord all the time, not even with legitimate issues if you can avoid it. It is better to pay $100 to fix something than call your landlord to fix it for free. Remember, if you set everything up right you should be saving a lot of money each month compared to a residential rental anyway. You want your landlord to forget you are there except when he receives your check. Even if your landlord could send a contractor to fix something in your unit, you do not want someone poking around in your unit unnecessarily. Fixing an air conditioner on the roof is one thing but working on plumbing is something too intimate. Make sure you are able to do basic carpentry and electrical work or are willing to hire someone to do it for you.

Why Live In An Unconventional Space?

There are many advantages and disadvantages to living in a commercial space. These should be carefully considered when choosing your location.

Pros

Space is a huge benefit. This is the number one reason, with the possible exception of cost, that people choose to live in commercial spaces. If you simply want a larger space or if you need space for art, woodworking, metalworking, engineering or other projects, then a warehouse space is much better than squeezing into a one or two car garage.

There are financial benefits such as reduced rent compared to residential rent, and commercial space often has trash pick-up, sewage and water included. No HOA dues either. You will cut your expenses greatly by having one large location instead of a small home and a small affordable office.

You no longer have to drive to work if you have your own business. Wake up and you are there.

Utility costs are reduced because you may have a smaller space to heat and cool. You can use a smaller and more energy-efficient oven. When we think of a kitchen, we usually think of a big stove. Most people do not need a big stove. If you live alone then you are unlikely to ever use more than one or two burners at once. This means you do not have to deal with installing a big bulky stove in your commercial space. A small countertop convection oven uses half the electricity of a full size and does not require a 220V outlet. You can use a hot plate for your stove-top cooking needs. It can be tucked away on a counter when not in use and they are so cheap you can get a second for the times you need a second burner. The small oven and two hot plates will cost much less than a full-size stove.

If you build your kitchen and bathroom in a modular way, as I describe later, and realize you do not like where you live, you can move into a new area very easily. You can disconnect your kitchen and shower and carry them to another commercial location, making the conversion to a livable space easier the second time.

There are advantages to isolation, too. Some personalities will thrive in the combination of total isolation at night and the hustle and bustle of the daytime activity.

Living in a commercial space is also a benefit for your neighbors. You can call the police if you hear a disturbance or break-in or see something fishy after hours.

If you do it right, bad neighbors are easily avoided. Blackout or otherwise obscure the windows, as I will describe later, and put a video doorbell on your front door. Keep it locked and do not answer it unless you are expecting someone. Voilà, no contact with neighbors. If you do not leave the front door open, leave the roll-up door open, or hang around outside then you never have to deal with neighbors asking any questions. One of the things I like best about my location is no obnoxious neighbors. Neighbors are usually busy running their business and they leave at the end of the business day. They rarely have time to bother me.

Cons

Commercial spaces do not have live-in ready bathrooms or kitchens. You will have to build your own kitchen or add to an existing kitchenette. You will have a bathroom in most locations but it will not include a shower. There are many options for adding a shower which I will explain later.

In a residential area you can complain if someone is playing music late at night. In a commercial area there is no ordinance that requires quiet after a certain hour because it is expected that businesses may run night shifts. Your neighbor may have a garage band and they may practice after work hours until 2 AM. You cannot complain as long as it is within the zoning rules. You may have a neighbor who works on car stereos so you have to listen to thumping bass day and night, or he tunes engines so you listen to racing engines all the time, or a neighbor who uses a loud PA system all day or some other industrial machine that makes a lot of noise. These issues are avoidable. Make sure you spend some time in the area you are planning to move to. Visit the location at different times of the day and night. Walk around if you can to see what the place is like. There is always a risk someone noisy may move in next door after you move in, so picking a stand-alone building or the corner space of a larger building is always preferred.

Dogs, cats, or similar pets that can cause any smell may be prohibited. It is also going to be an issue if your pets require walking. My advice is, if it does not fit in an aquarium, don't get it. The only exception is if you are actually running a business that involves animals, making it normal to have dogs or horses around.

Be prepared for only one bathroom. Large office spaces may have a women's and men's bathroom. Most have only one. Commercial offices have bathrooms that are required by law to be handicapped accessible. This means there is usually enough room in front of the toilet for a wheelchair and this spot makes a great place to add a shower. You can use a self-standing shower or one of those step-in tubs for the elderly that is upright. I will discuss how I added a shower later.

Another downside is that you are responsible for repairs. Commercial leases routinely make the tenant responsible for everything that is not structural.

You cannot register to vote using a commercial address unless you contact the election commission and notify them you are in a live-work space and this is your only residence. If you file your voter registration using a commercial address, it will likely be rejected.

Legal Considerations

If you have not read the disclaimer at the start of this book then read it now. I am not a lawyer and am not giving legal or accounting advice. The following is based solely on what I heard a couple of guys who looked like lawyers discussing in a dark and smoky bar one night. The laws in countries other than the US may vary and they can vary from state to state.

The magic phrase to open up a commercial space for residency is "live-work artist space." Many cities allow live-work exceptions for artists because artists do not keep regular work hours and need lots of space. Live-work zoning exceptions are often allowed for artists, such as the M1-5a/b zone in New York.

When I picked my commercial space, I had the benefit of knowing the landlord from a previous rental. I was able to secure the location as a live-work space for artists. This may not always be possible and you may not want to bother trying. If the landlord thinks renting to you is going to be a hassle then the landlord may turn you down flat.

You cannot "live" in a building zoned as industrial or business. However, it is not always clear what that means. If you work until midnight, then lie down on the couch for an eight hour nap, then get up and wash off, change clothes and go back to work, are you "living" there? As long as you go somewhere else... eventually...in my opinion, you are not "living" there.

This does not mean you have to rent an apartment or own a house that you visit occasionally. The definition of residence is not always clear and many courts define it on a case-by-case basis. You could officially live with family as long as you can throw a futon on the floor somewhere in their house or with a girl/boyfriend. You could even live out of a hotel. Many people live temporarily in hotels and some hotels have monthly rates with people living there as their main residence. How many business travelers fly to a distant city, spend six months "living" in a hotel when they really spend most of their time in a client's office working well into the night and even napping there?

To avoid making the office space look like a residence, you only have to act in a way that is appropriate for the location. Avoid disturbing the neighbors, keep the appearance of a business or storage warehouse and generally blend in.

If you do not have an official live-work designation from your zoning commission or the property is not already zoned as live-work, then you want to keep a place you "live" in mind if anyone asks. You can say, "I live with my parents, six states away, but my business is here," or "I am going to a hotel tonight and 'live' there." You can even say "I am homeless so I sleep in my car; you don't discriminate against the homeless, do you?" How are they to prove on the spot that you do not live with your girlfriend, your parents, in a hotel, or in your car? Unless an inspector or the landlord has it out for you, or you are causing problems, they are unlikely to ask any more questions or follow up again. Just saying you work late at night or that you have clients on the opposite side of the world and have to be in the office to conference with them during their business hours is usually enough.

Most zoning codes for industrial/manufacturing spaces allow one caretaker or security person to live on the premises but only in a special space reserved for just this purpose, and there are limitations on the size. If you buy a space or rent and are the only one on the property and that property is not connected to any other buildings, you may be able to use the caretaker/watchman loophole. So what is a "living area" for a caretaker? You need a bathroom, kitchen and bedroom so that is your living area. That means the rest of the property is yours to setup an employee rec room(living room) and warehouse for anything you want. This will not work if you are renting a space in a large building divided up for other tenants who rent similar spaces unless you can get the landlord to agree to make you the official caretaker. California zoning rules commonly include statements similar to: "Caretaker quarters in the M1 (light industrial) district consisting of permanent quarters for a guard, custodian, or caretaker are permitted in the M1 district when incidental to a permitted primary use. These include some space limitations on the living area." This exclusion can sometimes be used but check your local codes for details.

I have never seen any zoning rule that clearly defined what "living" meant. If you sleep over one night a week in your office is that "living?" Two nights, three out of seven, six out of seven nights? Most people will likely spend at least part of one night a week away either on a trip, on business, or with a girl/boyfriend so my interpretation is that if you do not sleep on premises 365 days a year, you are not completely living there. How can a zoning board declare that someone who works until midnight must drive home even if that person is drowsy and would be unsafe on the road because they are not allowed to take a nap for a few hours on the couch of their office? There is no way they can require you to do something unsafe so no way to prohibit you from sleeping in an office.

Some codes have an exception for employee recreational activities and facilities.

I consider sleep a recreational activity which therefore requires a facility.

Some areas let renters live in their office but state it cannot be converted to a residence, so no actual kitchen or full bathroom. This rule applies to the landlord and not necessarily to the tenant. They cannot prohibit a shower because you may need to wash off oily mechanical parts or need a shower as a chemical safety shower. A shower also does not have to be in the bathroom. They cannot prohibit a kitchenette if it is part of a break room and has reasonable facilities for that purpose such as a microwave, small toaster oven, refrigerator and sink. Remember what I said about not using a large oven? Here is an important reason that you want to use a smaller toaster oven. Having a big oven and dishwasher makes a kitchenette into a kitchen. Having a room with a microwave, toaster oven, hot plate in a drawer and refrigerator is always a kitchenette for a break area. It would be illegal for your landlord to convert the space to a living space and then rent it out as such, but it is not illegal for you to make these changes in most areas.

There are places offering special artist lofts as live-work areas. These areas usually have long waiting lists for artists who want a space. They may have a tiny bedroom in a loft area and a small kitchen and large work area downstairs. Artists can get lower rents because these units are often in commercial or industrial areas which cannot be rented as residential. These spaces usually have a long list of people who want to rent so it is nearly impossible to actually secure one of these locations. They are the ideal live-work space because they are legally designated as live-work areas. The problem is there are not enough of them and they can be as expensive as a regular apartment or house rental.

Business eviction is different from residential eviction. Commercial tenant law and residential tenant law vary substantially. Statutes protect the rights of residential tenants who will be eating, sleeping, and raising families on the property. Commercial tenants are treated as if they have more bargaining power and therefore have fewer legal protections. This difference is not significant if you pay your rent on time and do not cause problems.

Commercial property is often more difficult for the landlord to rent. There is frequently a glut on the market and finding a business that needs a specific space is not always easy. This is very beneficial for you if you pick properties that are on the less desirable commercial side. These are perfect for live-work spaces. If you rent a less desirable space that the landlord has not been able to rent for years previously, that landlords wants to keep you in the space if you pay the rent and you are not causing problems. The landlord is likely to overlook suggestions by neighbors that you might be living there in such cases. Eviction is only an issue if you do not pay rent or cause big problems.

If a landlord does want you out of a commercial space the rules are different than for residential eviction. They vary from locality to locality, but I will give some general guidelines. Commercial tenants may receive only three days' notice of eviction. The landlord cannot evict tenants by changing locks or canceling utilities and not by removing personal property to force the occupant out. These rules apply to residential rentals too, except for the notice requirement. Notice can be 30 to 90 days. A landlord cannot evict you from a commercial space without giving adequate notice first. You do not have to move from a residential rental immediately and must either move on your own or come into compliance with whatever the landlord dislikes. Getting rid of a barking dog, paying back rent, or whatever the landlord dislikes can be fixed to bring you into compliance in a residential rental. If the problem is not resolved, the landlord then files a lawsuit to evict you and the landlord must prove you did something that violates the lease or otherwise justifies ending the tenancy.

In commercial rentals, a landlord can issue an *Unconditional Quit Notice*, which means get out, no negotiation, after repeated violations of a significant lease

Keep your reception office looking like a professional business office that is actually being used for business.

agreement clause. This may include being late with the rent multiple times, causing damage to the space that is serious, or engaging in illegal activity on the premises.

Other notices are the *Pay Rent or Quit*, which means what it says—pay rent in a week, or get out. *Cure or Quit* means cure a misbehavior or violation of the lease or law in a specified time or get out.

Just as with residential rentals, the landlord can ask you to move out even if you have paid your rent and not violated any clauses. Sometimes the building is sold or the property will be rezoned and rebuilt. This is very rare for

Kitchenette with microwave, refrigerator and sink.

commercial property. The landlord can send a 30 day notice to vacate or 60 or 90 day in some places. If your lease has expired and you are on a month-to-month plan, the landlord can do this anytime without providing a reason. If you do not move out, the landlord files the eviction lawsuit and serves you with a summons. Rent control areas have other exceptions. Commercial spaces are not normally subject to rent control laws.

A three-day notice to vacate can be sent by commercial landlords if you do not pay rent one month. In reality, they will never do this because they want you to pay the rent and understand that sometimes a business that operates from month to month can have a bad month. In such cases, they should charge a late fee and accept the payment when it is made. As long as you do not go past three months of unpaid rent, there should not be a problem other than the extra fees you ultimately have to pay. If this does become an issue, be proactive and contact your landlord before he wonders where your rent payment is. The only time a landlord may want you out is if he has other renters who want the space at a much higher rate, and that is not a common scenario.

You can fight the landlord by pointing to errors in the filing of the eviction notice or in the original Quit Notice. You can also bring up any illegal behavior by the landlord. Show any cellphone video of the landlord acting aggressively or irrationally that demonstrates bad behavior, indicating bad-faith in his filing. Illegal behavior can include not maintaining the property or turning off utilities, which may indicate the landlord is trying to evict you in retaliation for demands the property be made habitable.

Unlike in residential rentals, a tenant cannot stop paying commercial rent just because there is some issue that needs repair or attention. A hole in the wall of a residence that goes unrepaired may justify withholding of rent or even abatement of unpaid rent during the time a significant issue existed that causes the residential renter to live in an unsafe, unclean, unhealthful space or one subject to outside crime unnecessarily. In a commercial setting, the tenant will usually be responsible for such a repair unless it is a major structural issue. Commercial renters will have to continue paying rent even when filing a lawsuit against the landlord.

A right to privacy is guaranteed in California and other places to renters of residential spaces but not to commercial spaces. This means the landlord can drop by anytime or otherwise inspect the premises. They can even use a passkey to access the property when there is no emergency or maintenance needed. This is almost never a problem because landlords usually have many commercial spaces to manage and do not have time to drop by and conduct random inspections. If you have a camera system, which I discuss later, then you can always catch such behavior if it occurs.

Commercial tenancies in most areas are viewed the same as any other arms-length transaction between commercially sophisticated entities. In residential tenancy, it is often assumed by law that the renter is not sophisticated and therefore requires more protections.

If there are any privacy violations by your landlord or a landlord representative, even if not legal violations for commercial property, or any other violations, always notify your landlord in writing or in a follow-up letter after a conversation. Do not rant but simply give the facts and calmly state the procedure you would prefer for entry to your business. This gives you evidence of the incident and that it was discussed. If you later need to take legal action then you are better prepared.

As long as you are paying your rent and not causing problems the landlord is not going to kick you out because they want a reliable rent payer and are not concerned with the business or whether or not you spend three hours, eight hours, 16 hours or 24 hours in the space. There is no difference between running two 12-hour shifts and one person being there for 24 hours. If you are paying your rent on time, not calling the landlord for problems to be fixed constantly, not having wild parties all the time, all you have to say is, I work late at night and sleep over sometimes. No further explanation is needed.

For insurance purposes, a primary residence is usually defined as a place you live for nine months out of the year or at least 50% of the time and is considered primarily owner occupied. This seems like a definition but is still vague. What is "a place you live for nine months?" Are you required to document 6480 hours were spent within the walls of the place? If you are working in the day and partying at night then you may only spend eight hours sleeping in your "residence," which is 2160 hours over nine months. OK, this is getting silly, I know. The point is that you are not required to have a time clock by your front door to check exactly when and how long you are "living" there. There is no statutory definition for principal residence in the Tax Code of the US. The IRS does not even use the term primary or principal residence and instead says "main home." A main home depends on the circumstances of the case and the good faith of the taxpayer. It is simply too complicated to lay out hard and fast rules to define a primary residence.

A general rule of thumb is that your primary residence is where you have your driver's license, car registration, voter registration and tax information sent. So, don't have those sent to your commercial address. Get a private mailbox and have them sent to it or to a parent's house.

You may have to continue paying a commercial lease even if the space is damaged by fire or flood. Even if the space is unusable for your business, you will still have to pay rent unless the lease says otherwise.

Any late charges should also be spelled out in your lease. If they are not listed in an exact amount or percentage, then you may be subject to excessive late fees. Such excessive fees are illegal in residential rentals but not in commercial rentals. Make sure any extra fees are clearly spelled out.

Keep in mind that no commercial lease provides a right of habitability. Even if you have a live-work space clause in your lease, it may allow habitability but not require the landlord to provide a habitable space suitable for living.

Beware of Estoppel Certificates. An Estoppel Certificate gives a third party information on the relationship between the tenant and landlord. This third party may be a person or entity interested in purchasing the land or building. It may also be for a lender who is reviewing a loan secured by the property. These certificates are part of due diligence to show a third party that renters exist and are paying rent. The general wording is to confirm that certain things about the property or rental relationship are true. These certificates must be signed and this can alter the terms of your commercial lease. Another risk of signing these is that if any statements you mark as true turn out to be untrue, you may now be liable to the third party because you certified they were true. It "estops" or prohibits itself from claiming a position different to what is stated in the certificate. Therefore, you must make sure the statements you agree to are true and not overly broad. You especially want to confirm that they do not include things you could have no knowledge of such as past defaults by the landlord. Try to include a "to the best of my knowledge" line somewhere in the statement. Leases may specify that if the tenant does not respond within a reasonable time, the landlord can sign the Estoppel Certificate on behalf of the tenant. You want to either respond or extend your time if you are in the process of renegotiating a lease. An Estoppel Certificate is not a commonly used tool in commercial rentals so be very careful if you are asked to sign one, and have a commercial real estate lawyer review it first.

Hiding a sleeping area is not difficult.

Most commercial warehouse spaces are in large industrial/ manufacturing complexes with multiple tenants.

What if you get caught?

Finding the perfect space that is already approved as a live-work rental is going to be very difficult. Convincing a landlord to let you live in a commercial space is also not easy even if you get zoning board approval in advance. The reality is that most people who live in commercial spaces are simply going to move in and keep a low profile without the live-work exemption.

Even if you don't go to the zoning board and request a variance to allow you to live in a commercial space legally, and you get caught living in a commercial space, there is little they can do. What is caught? How can they prove you live there? Unless you have three kids and a wife and sit in a lawn chair in the parking lot drinking beer every afternoon, there is no way to prove you live there and not in a hotel or with relatives or a girl/boyfriend or that you don't live in another city and simply sleep over when you are working. As long as the interior looks like it could be a workspace, which I will cover later, then it is difficult to prove you are living there. Even if you tell everyone you are living there and the zoning board or landlord finds out, you will get a notice to stop living there or possibly a small fine. So you move to a hotel for a little while or move in with friends, pay the fine, problem solved. Move back in a few weeks later and keep a lower profile.

If the landlord knowingly allows you to live there, not only is he breaking the law, he's also violating his insurance policy and opening himself up to legal issues. If, instead, your landlord can pretend he is ignorant then he will not care as long as you are paying the rent and not causing problems.

The IRS may not agree. If your company is not a sole proprietorship then you may need to pay the rent from your personal account and take a home-office deduction. If you have a corporation or LLC that pays for the rent and you live there, that could be prosecuted as money laundering because you are using the company to pay your personal rent with pre-tax company money and that is not legal. This all comes back to proof that you are living there and not with a girl/boyfriend or with family, which can be tricky to prove.

Live-work arrangements are not something property owners want to deal with because it might mean their tax status changes to mixed use instead of the less expensive (or more expensive, depending on your area) commercial use. If the landlord thinks you may threaten that status he may want you out. If that happens, move to a hotel for a few days. Unless the landlord sits out front and notes when you come and go, he has no way of knowing if you are living there or working late.

If you buy a warehouse, live there for a long time, and then are caught by the zoning commission, they may want a lot of back taxes. But then we are back to the question of how do they prove you lived there and not with a girl/boyfriend or with your parents? As long as you do not tell everyone you live there then there is no problem. Just say you work there a lot late at night.

> If spaces are too expensive in your city, check surrounding cities. Smaller surrounding cities often have lower rents. Rents vary. Not all commercial space is cheap and not all residential space is expensive. The benefit of cheap commercial space is that it is not in a bad neighborhood, just in an area with too many commercial spaces or in a retail area that is inconveniently located.

If there is any problem, you always want to be able to prove you do not live there. That is simple enough. Move to a motel. If your place is set up correctly, nothing in it should scream that you are living there. If you make the sleeping area so the bed can be hidden, the kitchen and living room look professional and the front office reception area has a computer, desk, phones, and filing cabinets, it looks like an office.

I made the reception area my main office with a desk and computer. This is what anyone entering through the front door sees. I put a bed in a separate side office and covered the windows with white plastic sheeting so light comes in but no one can see in the room.

I use another larger office as the living room but it looks like a conference room because I have several office chairs in it, a large screen TV and a conference table I can fold up when it is not in use. I picked up the office chairs cheap at yard sales. My kitchenette has a table for eating, a refrigerator and microwave sitting out. Everything else is in cabinets. I do not keep food out or anything that screams personal kitchen in view.

My bathroom is a regular commercial bathroom with a shower added. My shower has an emergency safety sign on it, but it can be used anytime as a regular shower. It was built out of PVC pipe and decking lumber. The warehouse area is used for storage and business or art projects. Other than the shower, there is nothing the average person would see coming into my space that would indicate anyone lived here full time instead of simply spending a lot of time here working. The shower is easily enough explained in that I sometimes need to shower and change into a suit to meet clients, which is also completely true.

Your landlord may be OK with you living there, but if you ask permission you put him on the spot and he either has to approve something in violation of the zoning code, which means he breaks the law, or he rejects it which means he tells you that you have to move out. You may see the disappointment on his face as he tells you this because he may have known you were living there for a long time but never said anything because nothing needed to be said. By telling him, you have limited his options. He liked the arrangement with you paying

> Some office rentals are all-inclusive and include Wi-Fi, internet, water and even electricity.

rent and not causing problems and now it is ruined because he can no longer deny he knew you were living there since you told him.

Do you tell the landlord your plan? Never! You are not being deceptive either. You are renting a space for your business or as an art studio. That is 100% true. Anything beyond that the landlord does not need to know and does not care about as long as it is not a violation of the lease that can cause the landlord problems or cost the landlord money. Notice that I did not say just a violation of the lease. If you are violating some minor term of the lease, but you pay your rent and cause no problems, the landlord will not care. In industrial areas they are often hard pressed to fill spaces so are not anxious to kick you out. They cannot get rid of a tenant and jack up the rent for the next family standing in line like they do in apartments.

If you are uncomfortable keeping your private life private and feel you must tell the landlord, then this is not an arrangement for you. The odds are the landlord does not care but by telling him you now put him in a situation where he must take a position. Do not say anything to your landlord, your friends, co-workers, anyone unless they have a need to know. If anyone asks just say it is a live-work

Many commercial locations include trash disposal.

space and that should satisfy their curiosity. If they keep asking questions look at them like they are crazy and give the same answer in a tone as if they just asked you why you had two bathrooms in a house.

If your landlord flat out asks you if you are living there then you may have to be honest and say yes. You do not want to lie about it. You can immediately offer to move out and temporarily relocate to a friend's house. If your landlord suspects but does not want to know, then he or she will not press you for an answer. It is more likely your landlord will say something vague like, "I heard you were sleeping in your unit," or "some of your neighbors think you are living in your office." Neither of these statements comes right out and asks if you are living there. They are not even questions, they are statements. This indicates the landlord does not want to ask the question directly and is hoping you will simply placate him or her with a reasonable explanation they can pass along to any nosy neighbors. You also do not have to give a flat yes, but can give a "sometimes," which is open to interpretation. If you are not there 24/7 365 days a year then you really do live there only "sometimes." If your landlord suspects but does not care, then he or she is unlikely to ask. If the landlord asks, then he or she may simply want to know what is going on to make sure nothing inappropriate is about to get him in trouble, and he may be happy to find out you are living there and that is the end of it.

I once rented a commercial space long before I lived in a warehouse. That old space had two annoying neighbors who would park a car in front of the office doors at night, blocking me from loading and unloading to my own office. I would often work late and in the evening this neighbor would go out to eat, then return and park in front of the door, which means he parked behind my car and I had only half the previous space to squeeze my car through when backing out, which was very annoying. There were three cars in the lot at that time of night—my car, which was parked in front of my office in the marked parking space, and two of the neighbors' cars, one of which was parked one space from mine and the other which was blocking my office entryway eight feet from the parking spaces. It was like one of those ridiculous commercials where there are only two cars in a huge parking lot and another car comes along and barely squeezes between them. I was parked legally, the lot was empty, and this guy parks right behind me because he was too lazy to walk a few feet from the marked parking area. He was also blocking the fire lane. One night he tried to change his car oil in front of the door and spilled it everywhere so for weeks my customers, employees and I had to walk through kitty litter he put over the stain, and track it into the office. This is not how to keep a low profile. This is how to annoy neighbors which makes them want you out. One night I came in to work late and made noise as my keys hit the metal door adjacent to the neighbor's office. Through the glass door, I saw my neighbor

business owner come out in his boxers from a dark back room to see what was going on and I knew he was living there. Since he was causing problems for me, I reported it to the landlord. The landlord called me the next day and said my neighbors worked with suppliers in Asia so stayed late to talk to their suppliers during China's business hours. That is why they slept there sometimes. Yeah, right. That was the end of it. I did not really care if they lived there, but I did care when they blocked my door and messed up the walkway in front of my door. My landlord knew the neighbors were living there but as long as they could give a reason for being there late he accepted it because he wanted them to keep paying rent and they were not causing him problems.

If you have a 9 to 5 job it can become obvious that you are living in your space if you leave at the same time and return at the same time every day. If you do have a job you must leave for, then it is likely to come up with your neighbors. If it does, let anyone who asks know your space is an artist warehouse or you run your own business in addition to working full time until your business takes off.

Is your landlord going to go to the trouble and expense to hire a lawyer, file for eviction, then pay a realtor to find a new tenant for a space just to get rid of someone living in the space who is already paying rent and not causing problems? It is very unlikely because he has no reason to get rid of a paying tenant and spend money to do it.

Make sure your landlord does not live on the property, too. It is a sure way to get caught because it will be too obvious you are living there if he is there all the time and can see you come and go.

If you tell your landlord you plan to live in a space, you likely will not get it unless it is already used as a live-work space or artist living area. As long as you keep a low profile and you do not brag about living there, nothing is likely to happen. If someone does complain, then we are back to the explanations already covered.

You can apply for live-work status through your zoning board if you get ousted and have to move into a hotel or in with relatives or a friend. This can be your Plan B, but if the landlord kicked you out, you cannot force the landlord to let you live there just because the zoning board says it is OK with them. It is better to have a place you can call "home" and spend all your time in your commercial space. If you keep a low profile and follow my advice, it will work.

What to say to the zoning board

You can go to your local zoning board and ask for a variance or waiver to use a space as a live-work space. Using it as an artist space is the best approach because you can explain how the artistic process works and how you need access at all hours when inspiration strikes and there is no difference between your leisure and working time. Many jurisdictions allow a space to be a live-work space if the user is an artist and anyone who has a camera is a photographer, anyone who can buy a paint set and make bad paintings is a painter, and anyone who can mold clay or work with metal is a sculptor. You have to be an artist. You do not have to be a good one. Another good job to claim is video editor. You can justify playing music and movies during the day or a personal theater because they are all clearly related to your "editor" job.

If they question your business plans, point out that if you have a sole proprietorship making and selling your art, there is no restriction on using your garage for a warehouse as long as it does not disturb the neighbors and you have a business permit. All you are doing is reversing this equation and instead of a small work space and a large living space in a residential area you have a large workspace and small living space in a commercial area.

Shipping containers can be turned into living spaces. They are available with insulation and even come in refrigerated units for temperature controlled shipping.

Look for a warehouse/office space with a roll-up door that allows you to park inside.

Picking your space

You will not find a live-work space using the keywords *live work*. If a space has an official live-work designation then they do not have to advertise because they have a waiting list. Spaces that are not officially live-work approved but are built out enough to be livable are rented on the down-low. You can ask artists about friendly places, but if they know of a place, it is likely already taken.

Commercial locations that are already set up for live-work but are not zoned for live-work are not advertised as livable. Look for keywords like *kitchenette* to find them. It is illegal for a realtor or landlord to offer a commercial space as a living space so you are looking at a "don't-ask, don't-tell" policy.

Some landlords or realtors will use keywords in listings that indicate the place is livable. It is a wink-wink way of saying you can live here and we will pretend you are not living here. Some phrases they use are "full bathroom and kitchenette for long-term use" or "suitable for an occasional overnight stay." Another sign of a landlord willing to have a *wink-wink* live in is when they show a photograph

Parking in an open lot is a dead giveaway that you are living in your space.

of a kitchenette sink in the listing or make a point of showing the break room and bathroom in photographs. This is their way of saying "look, you could live here" without spelling it out in the text which they are not allowed to do.

An advantage to most business locations is that they close at night so it is quiet. A disadvantage to a manufacturing or industrial area is that you may have extra noise during the day such as forklifts operating, people shouting, hammering or machinery working. You can't call the police and complain saying you are trying to sleep and your neighbors need to keep the noise down. You have to live with it, so visit the place you are interested in during the daytime and at night at different times to see what the noise level is like. Drive through the area at 10 PM on a Friday or Saturday night. Look for any vehicles that are obviously personal vehicles or multiple vehicles. Listen for noise or a band practicing. You want to know if your neighbors are using the space at night or if someone is already living in the complex. Personal vehicles parked in commercial areas late at night are a dead giveaway. You would prefer to live in a complex that has no one else living there, but this is not necessary. It is simply unwise to have someone else living there, especially if you are not in an official live-work space, because they will likely know you are living there just from seeing you come and go. If they cause problems and get kicked out,

41

Vacant lots or warehouses with no offices can be made livable,
but it is not usually worth the effort.

the first thing they will say is, "Well, Bob in unit 2 is living there, why do we get kicked out and he doesn't?" Even if you are not causing problems, the landlord may have to tell you to move, not because of anything you did, but because he cannot selectively evict people for living in commercial spaces. So even if the landlord suspects you live there and does not care, he or she may be forced to tell you to move. You can always temporarily move out or prove to the landlord that you work late hours and have a residence, which could also make the issue go away. Simply move in with a friend for a little while or live in a motel while making an effort to arrive in the morning and leave in the afternoon in front of the other tenants. You still "live" in your space but you temporarily sleep somewhere else. When things cool down, you can stop leaving at night.

Public health and safety are also an issue. You do not want to live down the street from or next-door to a business that uses hazardous chemicals of any kind.

Look in the newspaper, or craigslist.org, or Google for "commercial property City-Name, State." Some realtors post to commercial sites like loopnet.com and not to craigslist. You can also drive around industrial areas and write down phone numbers on for-rent signs to find real estate companies.

You need to be able to talk the talk when renting a commercial space. They will ask basic questions like how much space you need, what kind of business do you have, how many employees, how long have you been in business, are you a sole proprietor or a corporation. You need to be prepared to answer these questions and others.

You need to know the difference between a gross lease and a modified lease. You need to ask if there are community fees or any other additions to the listed rent. These are often called CAM or Cams. Listings that say "No Cams" or "No CAM fees" mean no community area management fees. CAM fees can increase rent anywhere from $150 to $600 a month above the advertised rate. Beware of any real estate agent who offers a low rate on a website and then tries to slip in that the rent is only for the first month when you meet in person. Do not trust this kind of agent! He has used bait-and-switch to get you on the hook by offering a low price and then admitting that is not the real price. It is unethical.

Part of talking the talk involves knowing how many square feet you are looking for. From your web research you should have an idea what commercial spaces cost in your area. You will most likely want a space with office and warehouse space. These are the easiest to convert to livable spaces.

Make sure you have enough office space so that the reception office can be made into a real office with your computer and look business-like. Confirm that the other offices meet your living needs. Make sure you have a kitchenette area or an area you can convert to a kitchenette. One nice thing about a warehouse is that you can build on if needed. Just add a room by building a floating wall that ties in to the existing offices. This is how I added a shop area to my warehouse. I built a floating room with storage above it.

If you need to add a kitchenette, you may want to wait until late night to do any noisy plumbing. Your neighbors might become curious if you make a lot of noise during the day.

Cover the floor of any added rooms with carpet or inexpensive interlocking flooring or leave it concrete. Your main air conditioner and heater should be able to heat a small addition. If it does not, then you may need to upgrade, at your own expense, the air/heat or add a heater or air conditioner to the new room. You will need permission if you alter the existing offices or structure but usually you do not need any permission to build something in the warehouse that does not alter the structure. Building a room that happens to butt up against the door that previously entered the warehouse does not alter the building and the new room can be torn down easily, so it should not be a lease issue.

My choice was an office/warehouse space, but I did look at a number of retail spaces too.

You can rent a large retail storefront with permission to sublet. Wall off a small front area by the windows to rent out while you live in the back. Tell your landlord you want the back for warehouse space and an artist studio but want to rent the front to a small shop owner. The result is you get a legitimate business up front and the back is all yours. The sublet business may pay a significant part of your rent, too. You may not want the subletting business to use your bathroom because their employees would have to come through your private living space. It is no longer private if strangers are walking through while you watch a movie. You may suggest they use a portable toilet for emergencies and completely lock the door connecting the front and back, telling them it is a secure storage area. You could make arrangements with a neighboring business, perhaps some trade of services, or let a neighbor put a sign advertising their business on your store window, in exchange for the subletting employees using their bathroom.

Blacking out the front windows of a retail space may look suspicious if no other space does the same in your area. An excellent alternative is to create

A display offset that fills windows can be used to keep the look of a retail store but hide the interior for privacy.

an offset display area. Create a barrier two to three feet behind your front display windows. This can be a movable wall made from painted foam 4x8 foot insulation sheets available at any home supply store and held up with simple brackets, or light-blocking curtains. If your barrier is carefully built to cover from ceiling to floor so no light comes through and you add a few lights to the front display space, you will be able to display products or artwork and no one can tell if you have lights on behind the display. For the front door, you can curve the offset display walls in or let them continue across the front door and hang a black curtain behind the door. You can black out the door but it looks like you are trying to hide something when doing this in a retail space. In an office, blacking out the door is not unusual. In a retail space it can seem odd, especially if you are in a high traffic area where a retailer would not want to keep people out. Using the offset area lets you actually offer items, display a sign with a URL where people can purchase products or art, and keeps the actual store area private for living and working assuming you do not plan to actually open as a business accepting customers.

Don't be afraid of a neighborhood that looks run down. Remember, you care about what is inside the building. You are not going to be walking your dog and chatting with the neighbors in areas like this. A rundown area past the edge of town that looks like it is ready for the zombie apocalypse is the best place because it means no one will be walking by or trying to peek in your windows.

Do not alter the outside in any way that might indicate that the building is not a warehouse or other commercial building. If you have a real business then a sign is expected. Otherwise, you do not need any. If you are an artist or living there only, then no signs at all are needed except for a no solicitors sign to avoid unwanted door knocking.

Make sure your space has some level of insulation. A warehouse in a cold or hot part of the country may not be capable of being heated or cooled in an affordable way. If you have a more moderate climate then this may not be as important. A moderate climate makes the warehouse usable year round. Roll-up doors usually are not sealed or insulated. Air will pass around them. You want a living area that is or can be separated from the warehouse area otherwise you may be hot in the summer and cold in the winter as air flows freely around your roll up door. This is another reason I prefer warehouse/ office spaces where the office is separate. You may have a smaller space with a garage type door that is insulated or sealed which is always helpful when it comes to controlling the temperature.

You do not have to rent a warehouse. You can rent a storefront. You may even find one where you can live upstairs and sublet the bottom floor. One of the best locations is a stand-alone building on the edge of town with little to no traffic and no neighbors. A stand-alone building has no other buildings or rental units attached to it. That means no nosy neighbors and no one who can hear you or your TV through the wall. I looked at a location like this when considering my move because it would have been an ideal space with a stand-alone building on the corner, large open retail space, air conditioned front area, roll up door in the back warehouse and super low rent. Retail spaces on the edge of town are often hard to rent, especially if they are not on a major roadway, so landlords may be happy to rent to you at any price.

Avoid office spaces that are shared or have restricted access. If you try to use an office which has a shared secretary or assistant, it will quickly become obvious to your neighbors or to security personnel that you are living there. Avoid any location that has security you have to check in with or that has a security gate monitoring your entry and exit. I would not want to live in a location that had a full-time security guard either.

Churches are great locations because they usually have many smaller classrooms you can use for offices or storage or bedrooms. A church can be rented but you will be high profile. Be prepared to admit you are an artist and if this is the steeple/stained glass kind of church, you may even consider an open house art show for the neighbors. This lets them come in and see that you are "working," What? You don't have any art? No problem, invite local artists to show their work. Your neighbors will see art and no one will be making a list of who painted what.

Check your local shipyard. An older location often has potentially livable offices or office/warehouses that the landlords are anxious to rent. You may have to deal with ship horns at all hours when ships come and go, but most of the time it is quiet. One problem with shipyard rentals is that the landlord may only want shipping-related businesses. These rentals may not be openly advertised so you may need to go to your local dock and look around if possible. I have suggested avoiding locations with security; however on a dock there may be people coming and going at all hours so passing through security may not be a problem.

Missile silos seem like a really great place to live, but they have some drawbacks. They are expensive because many people want them. They are a mess because they are underground and have been abandoned for many years. The rusty pipes are unusable. They are far from civilization so electricity may not be available from the power grid. If they have a water pump and well you will be

lucky if it works or you will have to make other arrangements for water. They are very remote. Silos can be built out to be luxury homes underground, but that is extremely expensive.

My approach for my warehouse was to keep the costs as low as possible so this was not even a consideration for me due to the remoteness and expense of a silo. There are other underground properties which may be easier to convert to a living space. Many websites offer these unusual properties, but they are usually for sale, not rent. My website blog at www.WarehouseLife.com has a list of sites offering missile and other underground structures.

An alternative living space option many do not think of is a hotel. Smaller independent hotels or motels often rent rooms by the month. I once rented a hotel for $350 a month when rooms were going for $30 a night. They offered this non-published special to keep the rooms filled. Prices have gone up, but there are still hotels that will rent by the month for rates equivalent to $20 a night($600/month) which is cheaper than any apartment I have seen. You have the advantage of someone cleaning your room, and water and electricity. Disadvantages are limited space, lack of privacy with the maid coming in daily, possible noise from other guests, no security for your car in an open parking lot, and you cannot modify the property.

Commercial shipping containers are commonly available on craigslist.org and through various websites from $1500 to $2500. These are the large, tractor-trailer-size shipping containers used on ships. If you can rent an open lot cheaper than renting a building, you could convert one of these to a livable space. You do have issues of water, electricity and sewage to deal with. Climate is a consideration and it would not be suitable for some areas unless you build in insulation of some kind such as foam sheeting, or build in walls and use fiberglass insulation. They are also available with insulation and even refrigerated units for temperature controlled shipping. Shipping containers may be a good choice if you rent a warehouse that has water and a bathroom but no offices. Warehouses like these are often cheap to rent. The shipping container provides instant rooms, are well built, and you can plumb and wire them from the existing lines. When you need to move, you can disconnect the container's water and power lines and have it transported to a new location. If you use a vacant lot, you will need a second container to park your vehicle in because you do not want it parked in the open.

Any space you choose should allow you to park your vehicle indoors. A vehicle outside becomes a signal to everyone when you are there and when you are gone. Not only would it be obvious you lived there to have the vehicle out all night, it would become a security issue because in a commercial area many more people are passing by than pass by in a residential area. Strangers who notice your car there as they pass through and then notice your car is gone when you are away for a vacation will know your place is not occupied and could take the opportunity to break in. If there are homeless people in the area or apartments nearby that can see your living space, they will notice when you are there and when you are away, too. Always look for a location that has a roll-up door or some way to hide your vehicle. It is even better to have a location where you can pull in and out without attracting attention.

In my building complex, there is someone else living in a space, but it is obvious he lives there. His pickup and his roommate's pickup are always parked out front instead of inside. This makes it easy to see they are there all day and all night because no other vehicles are used and these are clearly personal vehicles. Get a place with concealed parking.

A vacant lot or warehouse with no offices can be made livable with an equipped van, RV or Airstream-style trailer. Some areas may prohibit parking a trailer or RV in a vacant lot, but they cannot prohibit parking it in a warehouse. This arrangement may work if you need very little living space and a lot of working space. Some considerations are sewage disposal, electricity and water supply. These may be available with a warehouse but are unlikely with a vacant lot.

There are a number of people on eBay and other sites trying to sell California or other state coastal property cheap. They will tell you that you can build a home and have a beautiful ocean view. What they do not tell you is that this is a common scam. They sell the property cheap and when you try to get a building permit, you discover that a house cannot be built because the ground is solid rock and there is no way to install a septic tank or there are no access roads. This may sound like a dead end, but not necessarily. I will admit I have not done this, but here is an interesting idea. Find one of these cheap plots. See if you can put up a temporary or permanent service building by contacting the county courthouse or zoning commission and asking what restrictions are on the property. They may not allow a house, but may allow shipping containers to be placed there if they will be used as a weather monitoring station or antenna farm. You can buy weather station kits for under $100 to turn it into a real weather station. If you never get a client or FAA/FCC approval for your antenna farm, then it will forever be an antenna farm with no antennas. It does not matter if you never have a successful monitoring station or antenna farm if you really want it as living space. Some issues to check are availability of water, electricity, sewage disposal and access roads. Some of these places cannot have electricity run to such a remote location so you may have to use a generator or solar energy, have water trucked in or sewage trucked out. You can also find out from the county if you can build a service building with a bathroom. Have that built and signed off. Then you can add a shower, kitchen and amenities yourself. If you have solar power you can use a desalinization unit to constantly add water to a water tank from the ocean. Above ground septic tanks may be fine for one or two people. As long as you keep the outside barren and your vehicle in a container so it looks like a commercial building and not a home, you should not have any issues living there.

Malls are not a good choice for a living space. They will likely be too expensive because space is at a premium and you could not come and go at will once they lock it up. They also may have full-time security who would quickly realize you are living in your space.

Make a list of things you must have including a bathroom with a sink and commode, hot water, the number of rooms (offices), heat and/or air conditioning, and a room that can be used as a kitchenette.

You need a space you can use for a kitchenette that has either a sink or a place you can install one, and it should have a place for a microwave, toaster oven and hot plate. You can easily add a sink as long as plumbing can be run from the bathroom sink. You can be creative too. You do not have to use traditional plumbing and can use food-safe flexible water lines and a sump-pump to drain water back to the bathroom.

You will want a living room area. This can be a separate living room or a combination living room and bedroom. A small bed or a couch that converts into a bed can turn any room into a bedroom. A small bed can be concealed behind a privacy screen or a screen can be used to mark off a sleeping area in a larger room. A roll-away bed can be folded in half and tucked in a corner behind boxes or divider screens. I tried using a blow-up mattress. These are nice for visitors but they eventually leak if you use them all the time. Futons and Japanese roll-up type beds also did not work for me. They either do not maintain their cushion depth or are uncomfortable. I was planning to use a sofa-bed but already had a full-size bed so used it to avoid buying something new.

Do you need 220V power for your clothes dryer? Think about how you will clean clothes. You can always go to the laundromat, but that gets tiring quickly. You will want to think about where you would install a washer and run water and a drain line to it. You also need to consider where you would place a dryer. It has to be close to a 220V outlet and a vent hole for the dryer is necessary. You do not want to vent a dryer indoors. There are indoor vent systems, but they create a lot of back pressure for the dryer exhaust and reduce efficiency. The dryer exhaust puts out high-humidity air and small particles from the laundry, neither of which you want spraying in your living space. I placed my dryer near a back door. When I want to dry clothes, I push the vent hose out the door and bring it in when I am finished. I wait until late at night, after everyone has left, to do laundry. There are 120V dryers, but they are inefficient and can take a long time to dry clothes. If you do not have many clothes, this may work for you.

Is the space usable for your actual business or as an art studio? You want a space that you can make livable, but it also should be suitable for your business or for whatever other purpose you want to use it. It is always better to go bigger and than to go get a smaller space and realize you need more space.

Ask what utilities are included. Water? Trash? Is a gas hookup available or needed?

What about airflow? Can windows be opened or is airflow otherwise available? Do you need airflow or is an air-conditioning and heating system enough?

What about heating and cooling of your warehouse area? Do you need it heated or cooled due to your local climate?

Do you have 24 hour access to come and go as you wish? What about 24 hour guests? Can friends come by or is there a security area they must go through?

Is it private enough to live in? Are your neighbors going to be loud, such as an automotive service center that uses an air wrench or a manufacturing business that uses loud machines? Do your neighbors run a business that produces noxious fumes or use dangerous chemicals or produce smoke?

How noisy is the location during the day? How noisy or active is it at night? Is there a night shift? Avoid places that have night shifts or lots of night activity even if they are not loud. It simply creates a privacy problem.

Talk to neighbors where you are considering moving. You do not want to ask if the landlord is nosy but ask questions like does the landlord keep up the maintenance, and how often do they do inspections. You want to see if the landlord rents the space and does not bother tenants or if the landlord will come by to chat or have maintenance people do inspections randomly. Most of the time, the landlord rents and walks away unless something needs to be fixed or updated for building code reasons. You don't want them coming into your office/home anytime they want and if you have not shared that you are living there, you don't want them to see your bedroom. You can put an access control lock on the bedroom office so even if their maintenance people let themselves in, they cannot open that door without the code or key. Having a big dead bolt on an internal door will make them suspicious but a Simplex type push-button lock is not unusual for a business to have on a storage door.

Make sure your location includes trash pickup. Otherwise, you will have to sign up for trash removal and that will be more expensive for commercial spaces than residential. Most warehouse/office spaces include community trash removal in the rent.

Make sure you have control over heating and cooling in your space. You do not want to rent a place where you cannot control the temperature. The landlord may turn off heating or cooling at night, which would be disastrous for you. You do not want a heating/cooling control that is in another office or another unit where you cannot access it. Make sure you have your own heating and cooling system with a thermostat in your rental unit.

I have read stories from people living in warehouse or commercial property who complain about rodents, problems with trash disposal, no heat or cooling or loud neighboring businesses. These all come down to making poor choices on the location or the way they live. If you rent a warehouse that has no office space and is surrounded by homeless people, with a slaughterhouse on one side and a motorcycle service shop on the other, it should be obvious you will have problems. Exercise some good judgment when picking your location. Check it out during the day and night to make sure it is safe and suitable for living. In digging for more details in such stories, you will find that these people were not living alone but with multiple roommates who were messy and the real cause of rat infestations, or they tried cutting corners on trash disposal or simply did not know what they were doing.

One story I came across said there were 20 "artists" who were happily living in a warehouse and when the landlord found out they were all evicted. It sounds so sad when all the facts are stripped away. This was not the whole story. Some probing revealed the truth was that 20 hippies who were living in unsanitary conditions because they did not keep the place clean were evicted by the health department from a warehouse and they were all living in the same space. They were clearly causing problems for neighbors with so many people in one place, not keeping it clean, attracting rats and roaches so it is no wonder they were evicted. If it had been one or two people and they kept the place clean, it is unlikely anyone would have noticed or cared.

Avoiding eviction is easier if the stuff you own looks like it would be in a business, and personal items are stored in boxes where no one can see them. These 20 people obviously lived in the space and it did not look like they were conducting any business there.

Getting a place with an office area solves many problems with electricity, heating, and cooling because the office area is expected to be comfortable and livable.

Do your math first to make sure it is really the price you expect when you include insurance and utilities.

If your space does not already have a sink in the kitchenette, then mention that you want to add a kitchenette when first seeing the space. Most landlords will not object to you increasing the value of their property, but it is something you do not want to be a point of contention later. If there is already a sink of any kind then there is no need to mention it because the water lines are already run. If there is a bathroom then it should already have a hot water heater. The heater may be small, but even a small hot water heater is usually plenty for a shower or washing clothes or dishes.

Make checklist of things to do on inspection. Take a camera and make a narrated video because you will forget what it looks like after you see two or three spaces and you will likely always remember a place as being larger than it actually was.

Checklist

- Do you hear neighbors through the walls, then they can hear you.
- Ask how much insulation is between office spaces.
- What part is heated or cooled.
- Where is the thermostat and can you control it.
- What is included such as electricity or water and trash?
- Where is the bathroom?
- Is there a kitchenette or an area close to the bathroom plumbing that can be turned into a kitchenette?
- How much additional storage space is there such as overhead storage?
- What about internet service. Is cable or FIOS available in the space?
- Does the space have a roll up door where you can pull your vehicle in and once the vehicle is in do you still have plenty of space?
- Can you come and go freely or is there security or an access gate
- Can you blackout the front door and cover windows for privacy?
- Is the space adequate for your needs? Will it meet your personal needs and your business/artistic needs?
- What is the monthly rent, terms and deposit.
- Is there any damage, will it be repaired before move in.
- Will the place be painted and carpeted before move in if needed?
- Who is responsible for repairs and for HVAC repair?
- Are any neighboring businesses noisy or do they have noisy businesses like motorcycle repair with engines racing all day?
- Are you required to post a sign or can you just have a blank door?

Add your own special requirements to this list.

Before you move in, take photos and make a video walk through of the empty area, inside and out, so you have a record of any pre-existing damage or condition issues. Get close-ups of any problems. This may be useful when you move out if the landlord wants to charge you for old damage.

The Lease and Realtors

Commercial spaces are normally rented through realtors. The realtor handles advertising and all the details of the lease signing. Using a realtor shows that the landlord is experienced and professional and likely has several properties to manage.

Don't be afraid to negotiate. There are many spaces available. Even if they say no to your offer, if you walk away they may call you the next day and say yes. Ask for a reduction in the per square foot cost of at least a couple of cents even if it is already lower than similar properties. If it is higher, then don't be afraid to ask for a huge reduction that takes it several cents below market. Always ask for move-in time. That means you want the rest of the current month and the next month for FREE before your lease begins. It gives you time to move in, and most landlords will accept this rather than let the property sit unrented for another six months or more.

If you offer a monthly rent lower than the one requested and the broker comes back and says it was denied and then advises you to take the one offered, beware! He may not have even passed your offer to the landlord. Realtors get paid based on the value of the lease. They have little incentive to reduce your lease value by having the landlord accept a lower monthly rent. Any landlord should at least counter a reasonable offer.

The landlord will likely want a three or five-year lease. That is a common term for commercial rentals and it is reasonable if you get a break on the price and early move in. Read your lease carefully to find out if it goes month to month at the end of the lease. Find out what rent increases will be. Do not accept a vague description. The lease should spell out the exact numbers you will be charged in the current and following years through the term of your lease. If the base rent increases based on COLA (Cost of Living Adjustment) it should use the current year COLA as an example to show what you could be paying for the rest of your lease. If your rent does not increase, that is even better. If you renew your lease, negotiations are open again and you can ask that your rent be reset to the originally agreed amount. If there are empty spaces in your complex then you may get this reduction. If they do not want to reduce your rent, send a notice that you will be moving and make it clear that the rent is too high without the reset and it is more economical to move to a smaller space elsewhere. They may call you if they reconsider.

Beware of landlords who want to push you into a longer-term lease. If you are a multi-million dollar business renting a 100,000 sq ft warehouse...then they may want a longer lease. Any small business should expect two to three years. In slow economic times landlords will often try to get you into a longer lease so they know the space will be filled.

Beware of any realtor or property representative who is not able to meet you in person. This is a common scam where someone offers a property for rent which they do not have the right to rent. They may give a story about working out of state or being on a humanitarian mission in Haiti. They want to collect a security deposit and then disappear. Never rent a space without seeing it in person first.

Beware of impersonators. Landlord or realtor impersonation is very common on craigslist.org. You can check on the landlord and realtor and verify the realtor's license number. This person may have no connection to the property or may be the current tenant who has moved out but still has the keys or copied the keys and is pretending to represent the property. You may meet with someone claiming to be the realtor who introduces you to the "landlord," but they are working together. They obtained the keys from someone who has access to the building, or one or both are the current tenants who have moved out or were evicted, or they cut a key-holder box off the property door and took the keys out. They may have drilled out the existing lock and replaced it with a new lock so they can open the door.

Beware if you are shown a property that is different from the one in the listing. The scam works by listing one property and when you call, they give a different location and tell you the property you were looking at is no longer available. If it is not available then why were they listing it? The surprise property is usually more expensive, in worse condition, or smaller. The realtor may also be using the good property that is still available to attract renters and then take them to undesirable properties hoping to unload those first. If this happens, walk away. You should not trust a realtor who tries this trick.

Beware of a realtor who only has one property to show you. Legitimate realtors who represent commercial spaces have multiple spaces available. If a person claiming to be a realtor only has one space, that is a warning sign. He may have only one 100,000 square foot warehouse, but he should have several office/warehouse spaces of more average 2000 square foot size.

Beware of any realtor who asks for money early. Make sure you are dealing with a legitimate representative of the property. Asking for money up-front is always a warning sign.

Beware of any realtor who asks you to make a bank transfer, pay cash or Western Union/MoneyGram instant payment transfer. Certified checks or money orders may be requested when renting an apartment, but they are uncommon when renting commercial property. Your check usually clears before you can take possession anyway. Possession is delayed because you have to provide proof of insurance and the landlord usually delays while the space is painted and carpeted, until the check clears.

Beware of any realtor who wants you to pay a third party or make out a check to any business name other than the realtor's company or the landlord.

Beware of any realtor who is too anxious to make a deal and is willing to offer a deal well below market value.

Beware if you see several craigslist.org listings for similar spaces at one price and one listing with a price well below the others. The agent is listing a false price that only applies to the first month or does not include some made-up signing fee or the space has no bathrooms or offices, or is just a trick to show you a different place. They plan to make up the difference in hidden fees, or else something is different about that low-price unit.

Be careful of subletting offers. Make sure you see the lease and talk to the landlord before agreeing to any subletting offer. The tenant offering to sublet may be close to eviction. The person claiming to be the tenant may be someone who only works in the location and has no authority to sublet or has otherwise obtained the keys.

Your business lease will usually require you to have business insurance. You can sign the lease, but it will not be valid until your insurance company sends a confirmation certificate to the landlord. You will not receive the keys until the certificate has been delivered. Typical annual business insurance premiums should be $500-$900 for $1M total coverage per occurrence. That means you pay $500-$900 per year in insurance. This is for 0-2 employees in an average business that does not do anything dangerous. This is almost the same as I was paying for lawn mowing service when I rented a house so it is not that expensive. Any major insurance company can provide a quote for business insurance. Be prepared to answer a lot of questions about your business such as if you will have a monitored alarm system (the correct answer is yes) and fire extinguishers, if you will be using dangerous chemicals, if you will be renting the property out for events, if you do anything that could be risky. You always want to have a monitored alarm. This does not mean you have to buy an expensive monthly service. You can get inexpensive alarms on eBay or Amazon that will call your own cell phone number if they are set off, and that qualifies as a monitored alarm. You want fire extinguishers in the major areas too. If you will be hosting events or using dangerous chemicals then your rates will be higher or they will want more details about what you are doing and how much experience you have.

If you are an artist and do not have your own actual business, then tell your insurance agent that you are an artist and your business, (make up a good name), which is a sole proprietorship, is selling your artwork.

Remember, you should be saving a lot in rent compared to a similar residential space and that offsets the cost of the insurance.

The lessor will likely want a personal guarantee for the rent. This is normal if you are a sole proprietor or if your corporation or LLC is not a big, well-known name. When you sign a lease for an apartment or house, you are giving a personal guarantee anyway so it is the same thing. They may also want you to pay two months' rent as a deposit plus the first month's rent. Until you have a relationship with the landlord and they are confident you will pay your rent, they will want more up front. When you renew your lease you can renegotiate the deposit and perhaps have half of it returned or applied to the first month's rent of the new lease when you renew.

When negotiating, do so with confidence, as if you expect your offer to be accepted. If it is rejected outright, act surprised and say thank you and leave. If they counter and it is fair, take it. Once you have been in the space for one lease term and have shown that you cause no problems and pay your rent on time, you are in a stronger negotiation position when renewing the lease.

If you are not dealing with a property manager and instead the owner is directly leasing the property, this can become tricky. A property manager is used to dealing with repairs and usually represents a property owner who rarely, if ever, visits the property. Repairs are usually the responsibility of the tenant in commercial spaces, but major repairs or minor ones may be done by the landlord. Normally the plumbing and air-conditioning are still handled by the landlord. An owner who directly rents may want to do repair work himself to save a few bucks and that can be trouble in both poor quality work and him being nosy.

Always be wary of maintenance fees, especially if you are dealing directly with the owner. Such fees are not uncommon for spaces that have shared or community facilities, but they should always be clear and you should know exactly what you will pay every month. Never rent a property if you are told the amount is variable. If one tenant uses a lot of electricity or water and these utilities are included in a variable maintenance fee, it means the maintenance fee is distributed among everyone so you are paying their utilities. Beware of any lease that has multiple add-on fees or vague fees. A lease should state exactly how much you pay each month and that amount should never vary by the month. Any lease that includes occasional or unanticipated expenses is an attempt to defraud you. It is a way for the landlord to increase your rent when he wants more money. Such occasional or unexpected expenses can include salaries for the landlord or his property management expenses or staff, contractor expenses, repairs or renovations. If the landlord decides to improve a space he can then charge you for it even if it is not your space. You should not have to pay more because your roof or your neighbor's roof collapses or your landlord wants to take a European cruise.

Read your lease. Never assume. If you are unsure about anything, have a lawyer who specializes in commercial property rental look it over.

If you want to sublease part of your space, make sure this is spelled out in the lease.

Co-tenancy occurs when your tenancy is dependent on another business in the same complex or under the same landlord. The business you depend on is called an anchor tenant. The anchor tenant can be a known retail brand or a big manufacturer. You may rent a space next to a major fast-food place that brings in customers or rent a place in a medical oriented office building and your business sells to doctors who rush to you for last minute supplies. You may

rent a space in a strip mall where one dominant business draws customers in. What happens if the fast food place shuts down? What happens if the owner starts renting spaces to non-doctors? What happens if the dominant strip mall store shuts down and the customers stop coming? If the anchor tenant moves or goes out of business and it affects your business, you need a co-tenancy agreement to protect you from a potential loss of customers or from disruptions to your supply. Such an agreement allows you to break the lease if the landlord doesn't replace the anchor tenant in a specified time. If your business is not dependent on an anchor business this may be an opportunity. Look for strip malls or other business complexes where the primary business has moved away or gone out of business. The landlord will be anxious to rent spaces and open to making a deal.

Look for failed commercial locations. Many cities have sections where strip malls or organized business centers were built but the owner discovered he could not fill the spaces or the anchor tenant never opened. Maybe they were built on the edge of town or are hard to find. The result is a large group of unoccupied retail spaces. These are easy to identify because when you drive through there are no cars and all the buildings are clearly empty. This is another opportunity for the alternative living space renter to swoop in and get a good deal. First, ask the landlord if the space has to be retail. You can tell the landlord you are only interested in office space or an art studio. He will have little choice if all the spaces are empty even if he prefers retail tenants. If the landlord is obligated by contract or city ordinance to rent only to retail businesses, no problem! Get a business license from the city and a sales tax ID from the state. If you have a real retail business idea — GREAT! If not, then start a sole-proprietorship for some business you never intend to open and that requires no special permits or certifications. Normally you would not open a business as a sole-proprietor but if you are not actually conducting business and never open the doors to the public then you have no liability risk. You should have an idea what this business will be before meeting with the landlord or real estate agent so you can answer questions about it. Put a sign in the front window for your car alarm sales company, SEO consulting business or TV repair shop and never open for business. A business permit does not require you to be good at your business or make good business decisions. Anyone can open a TV repair shop and then be unable to hire someone who can repair TVs. The result is your business never opens. Now you have this nice space to live in and no one bothering you while you look forever for someone to work as your TV repair person. Do you get the idea?

If your landlord wants you to pay rent, his property taxes, his insurance, and his maintenance fees, this is known as a "triple net" (NNN) lease and they always favor the landlord. Never sign a triple net lease. Walk away. If you see a space advertised as NNN, you can always ask if they would lease it at the advertised

price but not under NNN terms. Make sure that your final lease does not have NNN terms in it even if they are called something else and make sure it lists exactly what the rent price will be each year.

When lease renewal time comes, do not just sign an extension or let your lease go month to month. Review the other spaces in the building. If you are in a multi-space building and there are many unrented spaces, the landlord wants to keep existing tenants badly and will give a good rate if you renew, or at least reset to your original monthly payment without the yearly increases which were automatically added. If the building is full, then the landlord may not be interested in giving a price break and you may have to continue with the current agreement or renew at the market price.

You do have obligations with a commercial lease that should not be ignored. There are people who sign a lease for a residential apartment or house and when they want to move just leave with no notice. They skip paying the last one or two months' rent, expecting to lose the security deposit while also hoping to avoid paying for damages, because people who do this usually cause damage beyond normal wear and tear and maybe scam the owner out of a free month. They often get away with it because it is easier to fix the damage and re-rent the property than for the landlord to pursue legal action and enforce the lease.

If you just walk away from a commercial lease, you are more likely to be sued. The person who signed as guarantor, probably you, will be liable for the remaining lease payments until a new tenant is found. The landlord is legally required to act in a way that mitigates damages, which means if you have two years left on a lease, the landlord cannot leave the space vacant without attempting to find a tenant and then try to collect the full two years of rent from you. The landlord must make a *reasonable* effort to find a tenant that is consistent with rental efforts of other units.

The landlord can't run an ad in the smallest circulation paper in town saying "commercial space for rent call 800-xxx-xxxx" and claim they are making an effort to rent your space. No one would respond to such a vague ad with no location, square footage or cost. Such an ad must be on par with how they attempt to rent other spaces.

If the unit is rented, you only owe for the time the unit was unrented. If the landlord has multiple unrented units then it is likely he will not find a tenant and will get more money by suing you. If the new tenant has a rent that is lower than your rent then you may still be held liable for the difference. This means the landlord can make someone a great deal to get them in and sue you for the difference. If the landlord is not motivated to find a new tenant or simply dislikes you and wants to make as much trouble as possible, the landlord may rent other units ahead of yours, show and advertise your unit but tell potential renters that the place has plumbing problems or that another larger unit is available for the same price. The landlord may advertise the unit but anyone who responds is taken to another unit which is likely identical or nearly identical, if you're in a commercial building with similar units. If you have a unique building, such as a corner retail building, then the landlord will likely not be able to use these tactics. If the landlord has an industrial or manufacturing center with many identical units, this behavior is possible and hard to identify. In this case, all the landlord has to say in court is, *"I have five similar units which are also vacant and I am trying to rent all of them out"* and the judge will accept that the landlord is not intentionally avoiding rental to gain the money from you. If you do need to break a lease, you want to survey the available units and you can always bring up in court that a previously empty unit identical to yours was rented a week after you moved out, which may show that the landlord acted in bad faith by not renting your unit out first.

Another option is to go to the landlord, tell him you need to move, have a job in another location, your business is not making enough and you are going out of business, or whatever the situation is, and discuss a buy-out option. The landlord may let you sacrifice the security deposit or pay anywhere from one to three to six months' rent up front and you move out immediately. The landlord may see money in the pocket as better than legal expenses or the remote possibility of collecting after two or three years of court battles.

If you are in a strip mall and it is empty (few or no other spaces rented), you could potentially argue that the landlord failed in his obligation to maintain the property by keeping adequate other units rented to maintain customer traffic. Some states have laws regarding percentage rental of malls or strip malls and landlord obligations.

If you want to stay in the location, you may find this abundance of unrented spaces desirable and rent an additional space to make livable. At this point you will have enough knowledge to convert a second space easily. Then sublet it to someone who also wants to live there. Repeat for each space you can get a good deal on, assuming you can find people to rent to for a profit and they will keep a low profile. You have an advantage here. The landlord cannot advertise the space as livable but you can informally connect with your network of friends and unconventional living people which gives you a higher chance of finding someone to fit the space than your landlord.

If you should need to move out, remember that you already have created a livable space. You can try to find someone else who wants unconventional housing and sublease to that person, even at a premium since the place is already livable due to your changes. Check your lease for subletting terms before offering the space to someone else.

If you are considering moving out, check with other businesses in your complex and ask if they need warehouse space or office space. You may be able to rent your warehouse area to one neighbor or your office space to another neighbor. One uses the front entrance, the other the back. Neither may have been willing to rent an entire space but are willing to split one. If you can come up with such an arrangement, the landlord may be willing to make it official with the other neighbors and cancel your lease. Even if you cannot get the full rent amount, if you can sublet the warehouse to a neighbor, that may help offset the monthly rent you are required to pay until the lease expires.

Dealing with a commercial landlord is different from dealing with an individual who is leasing a second home he owns. A commercial landlord is likely familiar with the legal system and has a lawyer on retainer to deal with suing businesses that do not pay rent. For them it is a common occurrence and simply part of business to rent a space, have the business fail or simply move out in the middle of the night, and have to sue to get the money owed.

You don't have a kitchen table, you have a break room table. Make a habit of using the terms office, kitchenette, break room or storage-room (you store your clothes and bed there, don't you?) instead of saying kitchen or bedroom. This will avoid slip-ups when talking to neighbors or anyone else who does not need to know the details of your live-work space.

I once rented a retail space for a business I started which was next to an empty storefront. A month after I moved in, a man moved a pet store next door. A month later, he was involved in a divorce, then a few days later I arrived at 8 AM to open up and the store next door was completely empty. He moved everything out in the middle of the night and skipped town.

If you want to move and your lease has reached the end and changed to month-to-month, review your terms. Usually it requires 30 days written notice but can be 60 to 90 days.

Ask for an inspection before you leave (after you move your stuff out) and walk through it with the landlord to confirm there are no issues and that you will get your security deposit back. It is not unusual for a manufacturing business to knock a small hole in a wall to run a pipe or electrical line, but it should be either done professionally or covered well. Something as simple as a piece of plywood screwed over a hole and painted to match the wall can be considered "repaired" by many landlords. It might not be acceptable for an apartment or house rental, but commercial rental tenants often expect to make changes, install phone systems or open walls so the landlord is not as concerned as he might be for a residential space. You can always put a vent or electrical outlet cover blank over holes if you do not have the skills to patch drywall.

Normal wear and tear cannot be deducted from your deposit. Normal wear and tear are more severe for commercial buildings than when renting a house. The landlord should not deduct charges from your deposit for repainting or new carpet. It is standard practice in commercial leasing to make these changes for each new tenant and not the financial responsibility of the old tenant. When everything is moved out, take photos of every room, wall, ceiling and floor, including any damage. Then turn on the video mode of your camera and do a narrated walk-through. If the landlord later claims there was major damage which was actually either minor or under normal wear and tear, you have evidence to contest his claims. It is a good idea to take photos and a video before moving in, too. This gives you a record of what the place was like. If there was a hole in a wall when you moved in, then you should not be penalized for it when you move out.

It may be cheaper for you to make minor fixes or replace broken items in the space before moving out. If a ceiling tile is damaged or an outlet cover is broken, the landlord has to pay a repair person to obtain the material and install it, which is very expensive. You may want to replace any bad ceiling tiles or small, easily fixed things yourself to avoid the risk of losing part of your security deposit. You do not want to be charged $75 from your deposit to replace a ceiling tile that you could have bought for $20.

What if your lease says subletting is not allowed and your landlord does not want to approve anyone? You are renting a business so you cannot be prohibited from having employees. Sublease the location to another unconventional housing enthusiast and call the person an employee or independent contractor. You can "hire" someone as a security guard. Then charge him to stay there. Now you can move out and your security guard pays you to stay there. You will still be liable for the rent and property. When you sublease, someone else moves in and pays the rent but you are still under a lease agreement and responsible if the person stops paying. Keep this in mind if you find a sublease or want to sublease other units. You always want to have your own sublease agreement signed by the subletting person.

Review your lease before telling your landlord you need to move out. It may have a simple bailout clause for either party to terminate. Commercial landlords understand that businesses fail and may need to shut down.

It is always best to have a legitimate reason to cancel a lease. Just walking away or falling behind without saying anything is more likely to be pursued in court than openly and honestly talking to the landlord to find a solution. If you just walk away or stop paying rent, then the courts will not look kindly on this no matter what reason you claim motivated you to stop paying. If, instead, you attempt a reasonable solution and the other side balks, it will at least be more favorable in court to you. Even with a contract, parties are expected to act reasonably.

If there is any breach of responsibility by the landlord that is substantive then you may have a reason to break your lease. This cannot be a minor issue, but must be a major issue that is ongoing. Check your local and state rental laws. It is unlikely this language is in the lease because landlords do not list their legal responsibilities in the lease.

Landlords are motivated to negotiate when they realize that a business may have a big sign saying "going out of business sale" on the front door. Even worse could be a "Bankruptcy Sale – Everything Must Go." A going out of business sign scares other tenants and potential tenants and makes it look like the location is not successful.

If you can find someone yourself to take over the space and who is willing to move in with no renovation, that is to the landlord's advantage because he does not have to repaint or re-carpet and gets to sign a new long-term lease. In this case, the landlord should terminate your lease and sign up the new person.

If you sell your business to another party, then the other party can now be assigned your lease agreement. This is also a common practice in commercial real estate. This may not even require a new lease but will require a two or three-page addendum transferring responsibility.

Filing bankruptcy can end your obligations for a commercial lease. You would need to go through a lawyer and discuss the pros and cons of this approach. It will likely be easier and less expensive to negotiate a buyout since you are not dealing with multi-million dollar facilities as a live-work space.

If you are moving out due to financial problems, first ask if there is a smaller or less expensive space in the same building or in another building controlled by the landlord. He may agree to let you move to another space at a reduced rent rather than lose you completely.

In a residential lease, if your landlord fails to maintain the property, you can maintain it and deduct the costs from your rent. Generally, if the landlord fails to repair your heating system, you can have it fixed, deduct the cost from your rent payment and include a copy of the receipt in your rent payment envelope. This is not always true for a commercial lease. Review your local and state laws for details on how this works in your area. Keep in mind, though, that many commercial leases are turnkey and once you take possession you are responsible for everything including lighting, heating and plumbing repairs. This is different from most apartment or home rentals where the landlord is responsible. Your lease will spell out what you are responsible for fixing.

After You Move In

If it quacks like a duck and walks like a duck...

You must look like a commercial or retail location or an art studio if you are living in a commercial building. You want to avoid making your place look like a private home. Today this is not too hard to achieve. There is nothing unusual about a company having a pool table or video games on site, a break room with a kitchenette, and a conference room (read a living room) with big screen TV or projector, (just substitute office chairs for a couch), and a storage or waiting room (bedroom). You can always say you are using part of the building for personal storage if anyone asks.

The bedroom may be the trickiest room. If you have a full bed and posters of rock groups taped to the walls, or the reception office area looks nothing like a professional office, then anyone inspecting the space will not buy your story about using the location for actual business. You can improve the illusion if you substitute for the bed a futon, Japanese futon, inflatable mattress, or sofa sleeper, all of which can be folded up and hidden during the day. You can even use the bedroom as a real meeting room and have clients sit on the hide-a-bed couch in a relaxing atmosphere to talk business. Throw some magazines on a side table and put a box of your brochures on the table that would otherwise be your nightstand and you have a legitimate business meeting room.

I converted an office to a bedroom. I planned to use a fold-out couch. I already had a full-size bed and did not like the idea of selling it for nothing and then buying a hide-a-bed couch so decided to keep the bed I had. I call it the storage room and put a sign on it saying Employees Only. I planned to shut the door during the day, but this did not work out. I would forget and anyone who walked by could see the bed. I did some rearranging to move the bed and closet, creating a maze entrance. Here I wanted to use office cubicle walls to make it look like a series of divided offices. I was never able to find affordable full-height walls that I liked. Since I could not get cubicle walls to hide the bed, I built my own walls using cardboard boxes. I glued them together and to wood backing strips to create faux box walls. They look like stacked boxes to anyone looking in the doorway. Only after walking in and through the L-shaped entrance can anyone see the bed and closet. This way any visitors assume the room is storage. If I really want to keep people out, I can stack empty boxes in the L entrance so the room looks like it is completely packed.

A faux wall is also a great way to hide anything valuable or personal. It hides what you do not want others to see and it is unlikely that a burglar would bother looking behind it if it looks like a stack of heavy boxes. It can even be used as a panic room.

Make sure that your front door looks like a business when someone walks in. Most people have home offices today. Set up your home office as the main front entrance. Anyone who drops by for business, or if the landlord or anyone else drops by unexpectedly, you can let them in and they will see your business office. Most of the time you will keep your door locked and not let in anyone you are not expecting. There will always be times when you need to let someone in who is not a close friend or family member and who does not need to know you have a live-work space. If you are an artist, the illusion is even easier to maintain because artists can have anything in the studio as long as it looks like a studio.

Artists keep strange hours so if anyone asks why you are there so late you have a reason, plus if a neighbor says he heard you watching a movie or listening to music just say you were relaxing before going back to work. You cannot realistically tell your friends you don't live there if you invite them over and it is obvious you live there, so tell them it is a live-work space, which is true. As for anyone else, tell them you work odd hours. You do not have to give any more information than that. If anyone presses you, then honestly say you do not live there all the time. This is true. If you spend one night a year away then you are not living there **all** the time.

Get a private mailbox (PMB). You want one to receive your mail and packages so you do not have to answer the door for small packages. If you do not answer the door then your neighbors will not know for certain if you are there or not during the day.

A private mailbox is also helpful if you move, so you will not have to change your mailing address for everyone. You can also get a post office box because you can use the street address for the post office as your physical delivery address at most post offices. FedEx and UPS will even deliver to your PO box. Your address is something like 123 Main Street, Unit 1111 where 1111 is your PO box number. Your post office will explain how to have packages sent to them. One problem with the post office is that you usually do not get packages the day they are delivered. If your post office deals with a lot of mail they will not process deliveries until that night so you will have to get your package the next day. With a PMB this is not usually a problem. If anyone asks where you live, just give your PMB address. If anyone wants a home and work address, you have both with your commercial address and your PMB.

Park inside. I said earlier that you should pick a space that has a roll-up door or some way for you to park inside so your vehicle is not visible. During the day you can park in front of your office, but at night park inside. Otherwise, your car is a dead giveaway that you are living there. It just does not look right to have a vehicle parked there all the time when your neighbors know it is your main vehicle. When everyone goes home and only one vehicle is in the

Faux Box Wall

Office cubicle walls were too expensive, but I needed to make my bedroom less obvious. I decided to make a fake box wall so it would look like the room was filled with boxes.

How to make a faux wall:
Cut the ends off several large boxes. Glue together to form a large wall. Glue wood strips to the back. This will give the wall strength and a way to make it stand up. Use the wall to create the illusion of a storage room.

I created an L-shaped pathway. Anyone looking into the room sees only stacked boxes. When I turn the corner I have my closet and bedroom.

parking lot at night and it is still there in the morning when people are coming in early or working late, they will know you are living there. My suggestion is to always park inside, day or night. If you park out front and your neighbors see you pull your car into your roll-up door after parking out front all day, they will be suspicious. If you always park inside, they will have difficulty telling if you are there or not. When neighbors see you leave at 2 PM, they will not know if you are leaving for the day or just running errands. When they see you pull in

When living in a commercial space always think in terms of using things for other than their intended purpose, accepting that junk is only junk when viewed through the narrow perception that it must only be used for what it was originally intended. I wanted a wood roll-top desk for my warehouse shop to use as a workbench. The $30 desk I bought was junk to everyone who looked at it so the seller was glad to get rid of it. It had stains from drinking glasses being placed on it and had been left outside in the weather, but I did not plan to use the desk as a fancy desk showpiece but as a workbench so it was no longer junk but a super fancy workbench. All I had to do was swipe some sandpaper over it and re-stain it. It was perfect as a workbench and much better suited to my art studio than a plain table.

Another opportunity to use things for other than the intended purpose came when I needed a better trash can solution. I hated having trash cans out where everyone could see them. They were ugly. I wanted a commercial style trash can like the ones used in restaurants,

but those are very expensive at $200 to $500 for one trash can. I searched cragislist.org and found an entertainment center for $40. I cut the top off, then cut two holes and cut the bottom off two stainless steel bowls I already had to make drop through trash cans like you see in coffee shops and restaurants. It looks nicer than exposed trash cans and gives me extra counter space. It holds two cans larger than I had been using and only cost me $40 too. I still have the bottom cabinet section to use for storage.

at 11 AM they will not know if you are returning from running errands or just starting your work day. If you have a personal vehicle and a delivery van, it is understandable to park the delivery van at your office and leave it overnight, but to have both there all the time is obvious, too obvious.

There are practical considerations involved in trash disposal, security, parking, cooking and bathing.

You want to be careful what you throw away. There are people who go through commercial dumpsters for anything they can use, or for recyclables. It is illegal in most places to take recyclables out of a dumpster because this is stealing. The sanitation company has contracted to pick up the recyclables at a certain rate and that rate is based on their expectation to collect recyclables that they will make money recycling. If people take the most valuable stuff out of the dumpster, then this alters what the company can make from their route. No one is supposed to remove items from the recycle bin, but it happens a lot. Homeless people will open trash bags looking for food. They may not complain about you living there, but if they tear open your trash bag and your neighbors go to throw something away or poke through the trash for something usable they will immediately see that your spread-out trash does not look like business break room trash but like home kitchen trash. The solution is to determine when your trash is picked up by the sanitation company and throw your trash away often and just before it is picked up. This means you are throwing away smaller amounts, even half bags of trash, that are easier to stuff down or less likely to attract attention.

I found the easiest solution to not having a stove was to purchase a hot plate. A hot plate is nothing more than a single electric stove burner. I bought one nice one, then a week later found a brand new one at the thrift store for a few dollars so I picked it up, too. I then had the equivalent of two stove burners and could cook anything I want. Later, I found a beautiful 1930s hot plate in my mother's attic so now I have three and can cook as much as if I had a full stove. I store them in a cabinet and only take out one when I need it. For my stove, I use a small countertop convection oven. It cooks everything I need and looks like something that would normally be present in a business kitchenette. I also have a microwave, which is normal in a kitchenette.

Do not get a full size 240V oven. If you are not cooking for a large family then you do not need it. If your business is cooking, then you have a legitimate reason to have a large oven. For a single person or couple, having a full size oven in your kitchenette makes it look too much like a kitchen and so should be avoided. Get a countertop oven. It uses half the electricity, takes up less

Make money from your extra space by renting it out to photographers, to incubator businesses, or as storage or a data center.

space and is far less expensive. That is all I need along with the hot plate. If you are someone who prefers gas for your cooktops, this is easily achievable too. If you have natural gas, you can find single hot plate style gas burners that have options to work with natural gas or propane. Most gas hot plates work with propane. The difference is in the nozzles that feed the gas. You do not want to use a propane stove on natural gas or vice-versa. It is easy to place a propane-fed single burner on a metal table and feed it from either a small or large propane canister. You have the benefits of a gas cooktop without the size or expense. Using propane can also save you from having a professional run flexible natural gas lines. A large propane cylinder should last you a long time. A small propane cylinder can also last a long time. The small green cylinders are usually disposable but you can purchase an adapter that lets you refill it from a larger and less expensive per unit volume tank. You can also use a propane camp stove.

Generally, you do not want to use propane indoors. Storing a propane cylinder in a residential area is not legal in most areas but this does not apply to commercial properties. I am not recommending that anyone use propane indoors. It is commonly discouraged due to concerns about carbon monoxide. These recommendations are generally based on using propane as a high output heat source that stays on 12 to 24 hours. They are not based on single meal cooking use, which is commonly 30 minutes or less. I have done my own research on the topic and found that propane produces relatively small amounts of carbon monoxide. If you are cooking for a short time and have

Storage Tip: If you have tall ceilings you can build a three to four foot elevated platform similar to a stage in your warehouse. This gives you a lot of hidden storage under the platform and you still have usable space on top. You can leave it open and use it as an artistic work space. You can add short, four-foot walls and turn the space into a bedroom. Once the room is elevated you do not need tall walls to hide the bed.

good ventilation, it should be safe. If you use either natural gas or propane appliances, get a carbon monoxide detector, which looks like a smoke detector and is usually available in the same area of the store. You want one that shows the PPM number on the display. This will indicate the smallest amount, long before it is unsafe or sounds an alarm. Use some common sense.

The refrigerator is easy. There is nothing unusual about a refrigerator in a kitchenette. You can get a small one or a large one and they run on regular 120V power. You can run a flexible water line if you want to use an in-door water dispenser or ice dispenser.

You will want a sink in your kitchen. If you can place the kitchenette close to the bathroom this will help because you have a short run for your water lines. You may already have a drain you can run to as well. If you cannot run a drain, you may need another sump pump to pump away the waste water. It may be worth hiring a plumber to install a drain, too.

The kitchen sink can be small, which is consistent with what is expected in a kitchenette. You can mount the sink in any table or yard-sale furniture. Just cut a hole, drop it in, run the flexible water lines and the drain. By placing the sink in a table or furniture, you can easily disconnect it and move it to a new location too.

You don't have to install a plumbed kitchen sink like I did. I used my bathroom sink for a month before I installed the kitchenette sink. You can also use a holding tank for fresh water and a 5 gallon bucket for your drain if you are unable to run a drain or water lines. Run a hose to fill the holding tank when it gets low and either manually dump the drain water or use a sump pump to empty it.

You do not have hot water this way but it will give you water and the same system can be used to feed a refrigerator water-in-the-door system. Similar systems are used at campsites where a water bladder is hung up and used for washing dishes or showering.

It is a good idea to have security cameras in a private residence or a commercial space. In a commercial environment it really is beneficial to know what is going on outside. You can see if someone is circling the area late at night or who is coming and going. You can see when clients or friends arrive too.

Some security systems have a phone app which lets you monitor your cameras from your phone. They are cheap and you will know if your landlord is spying on you as well as having evidence if employees or friends are stealing from you.

You can get super cheap standard definition (SD) security systems which include the DVR (digital video recorder) and several cameras. These are a good choice if you are on a budget, but the video quality is not very good and not even good enough to identify vehicle license plates. These are often advertised as 400 or 500 line quality. I recommend looking for a more expensive HD surveillance system with night video ability. You will get higher quality video and enjoy the system much more in the long-run. Many systems do not include the recording hard drive. A 250 gigabyte drive works for an SD system to record a week of video in some cases. A larger drive of at least 1 TB is better and they are not expensive. You can use a regular drive, but there are special video surveillance drives which are more robust and made for the constant writing that may cause a regular desktop drive to wear out or fail. Video does not have to be constantly recorded. These systems can be set to only record video when motion is detected which allows a drive to store a lot more video. You do not want to find out someone stole something a week ago and only have three days of video. Using motion sensors can potentially keep weeks of video activity for any given camera.

Camera systems can come bundled with four or eight cameras. Eight may sound better but you also have eight cameras feeding one DVR and eight cameras displayed on one monitor. It is better to buy two four-camera systems and then have two larger monitors so you can clearly see all the cameras. You could also

buy one four-camera HD system and one four-camera SD system.

Another option for cameras is a wireless nanny cam. These only require power and are a great option for those times when you cannot run wires but have power for the camera such as from a light socket. Use a light-socket adapter that gives you a plug-in. These cameras can sometimes have the receiver connected to your security DVR too. Wireless security cameras are also available.

Plan how many cameras you will need. One camera only covers a narrow range of about 80 degrees. If you get a camera with a fisheye or wide-angle lens the camera will cover more area but the image will be distorted and everything will look smaller or squeezed together. Plan on two cameras for each entrance so they can point in two directions and see everyone coming and going. Otherwise, someone who wants to break into your space, thinking it is unoccupied, may try to walk into the blind side of your camera and disable it. Two cameras will make this impossible to do without being recorded. You also want cameras on your non-private areas like the warehouse, car parking or other areas you want to monitor. These are better places for the wide angle or fisheye lens cameras because you can monitor an entire room with one camera. It is your call whether you want cameras in private areas like the kitchenette, living area or bedroom. You may want to monitor these areas in case of a break-in or if you want to keep an eye on friends during parties, or roommates. If something goes missing, you can check your camera. You do not have to use the bulky security cameras. Less expensive and smaller cameras are available that will

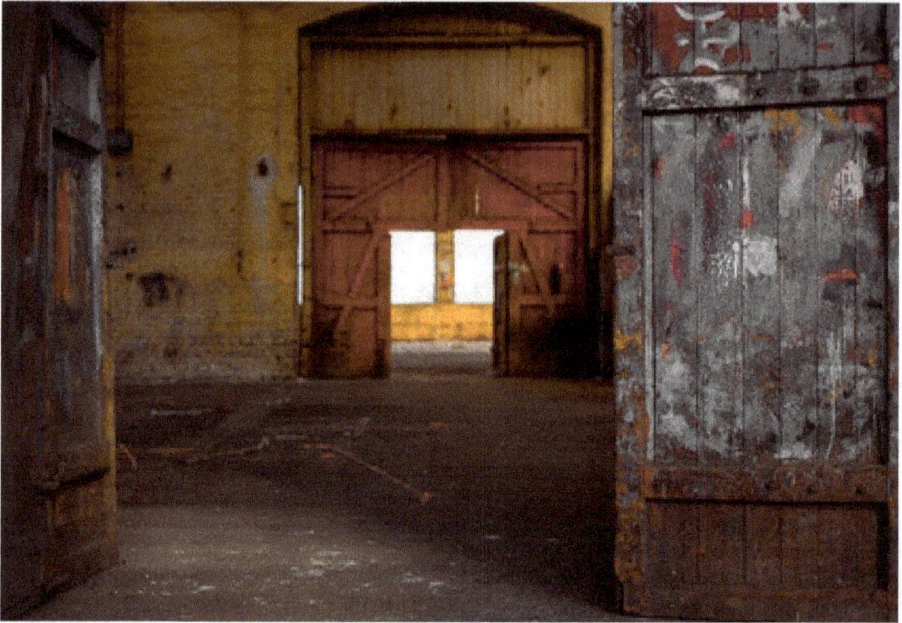

plug directly into the composite video port of SD security camera monitors. These small cameras often look like webcams or small black dots and are easily concealed. The car reverse cameras available for $10 or less can also be used but they will mirror the image and may have parking lines on the image.

Commercial offices rarely have closets. I purchased some closet organizer inserts and used conduit between them to create more cheap storage, then surrounded my closet area with Japanese room dividers. You can check craigslist.org for garment holders, wardrobe furniture or an armoire and closet inserts too. I used the room dividers because I wanted a large walk-in closet. They let me adjust the size of my closet easily. I put my closet inserts on casters. This allows me to rearrange or even collapse my closet if needed to really hide it well. If you do not need a walk-in closet, you can use the dividers like doors to hide the organizers along the wall. Did you know closets are a recent invention? People used to keep everything in trunks or wardrobe furniture. Homes were not built with full closets in the USA until the mid 1940s.

Originally, I wanted to use office cubicle dividers to divide off the bedroom and closets. These were extremely expensive so I went with the less costly room dividers.

Commercial spaces do not usually include a shower. Unless you are renting a location that was previously a gym, you will have to install your own shower or tub. I installed a shower because it was easy, more water efficient than a tub, and I can take it apart to move it if I decide to leave my location.

Commercial bathrooms are built to meet building codes which require handicapped access. Your bathroom will likely have enough space in front of the commode to fit a wheelchair. This is the perfect size to squeeze in a shower.

I researched freestanding showers but found none that I thought were usable. I did find one for under $200. It seemed flimsy and for the price I thought I could build one that looked nicer. I decided I was better off building a shower myself.

It is unlikely you will have a floor drain in the right place for your shower. If you do, that is great and you can use it. I had no drain so to drain the shower I decided to raise the shower up several inches and use a sump pump.

I built a base similar to a small deck with open slats for drainage. I placed a plastic storage tub under the deck. The storage tub stuck out one side where I placed an automatic sump pump. When the water reaches a certain level, the pump comes on and drains the water out a hose into the sink drain.

I used a T connector to connect the sump pump hose to the bathroom sink drain. I used the knobs on the sink water supply to turn off the water and attached additional screw-on T fittings to the hot and cold water. These were then connected by flexible connectors to PVC pipe that fed the shower faucets. This allowed me to install the water without even turning off the master water valve. I purchased a shower kit that included a thermal valve faucet system and the spray head all in one unit. This was mounted to an upright from the base and the plumbing was a matter of screwing to PVC threaded connectors. It was very easy and much nicer than the freestanding plastic shower I had seen. I then attached yellow and clear shower curtains to the sides. This created the walls and was very inexpensive. I can also change the curtains easily.

White or black plastic sheeting is an inexpensive way to cover windows. White lets light through and black completely blocks light. Large binder clips can attach it to most window blind mounts.

I made the shower look like a safety shower using PVC pipe painted yellow and a safety shower sign and yellow and clear shower curtains. This was a combination of aesthetics since I wanted the industrial look, and practicality. The design kept it from looking like a residential shower and it was cheap and easy to build.

I also considered putting my shower in the warehouse area. There is more room there, but I did not do this because the back is not heated or cooled. It would not matter in the summer when it is hot but would be very uncomfortable in the winter.

While I was building this shower, I had to bathe in something. For a temporary fix, I used a portable closet frame I happened to have. You can make a similar frame from ½ inch PVC pipe for under $15 and pick up a couple of shower curtains at the 99 cent store. I then used a pet washer as my shower head and connected it to the bathroom sink. The storage tub was large enough to hold all the water. I dumped the dirty water down the drain after each shower.

When I use my new shower, the sump pump kicks on automatically when it senses the water reach a level of about two inches. The sump pump can never drain the pan dry. The sump pump will leave about one inch of water in the bottom. This water will eventually smell just like a basement with a damp sump pump well. You can empty the tub once a week and let it dry. This helps a lot. Put bleach in the pan from time to time to kill bacteria. A cover with a drain-size hole also reduces the smell rather than leaving the top open and exposed like my installation. You do not smell a regular shower because the amount of water in the drain is so small and it is rinsed out each use. I found it easiest to get two pans and swap them out. Using two pans makes it quick and easy. While one was in use, the other could dry out and I can clean it anytime. This gives a dry pan to replace a smelly pan on short notice such as if you have guests coming over. The pan should be cleaned or changed every three to six months but more often is better.

My first shower design used a large pan that drained into a smaller pan with

Closet organizer inserts and inexpensive room divider panels let you create closets anywhere you want and of any size you need.

Portable toilets can be turned into a shower.

the sump pump. This caused the sump pump to turn on and off constantly. One problem I had was that I did not have a check valve installed. This valve should be installed as close to the pump as possible. It keeps water from flowing back into the pump. Without it, your pump will pump out, then stop, then the water in the hose will backflow, causing the pump to activate again, and when the level drops it will stop and the water will again backflow, creating a continuous on-off-on cycle that wears out the pump. Another problem I had was that my second container was too small. It would fill quickly and the sump pump would empty it quickly and turn off. Then the larger pan would continue to pour into the smaller one and the cycle would repeat. By switching to a single larger pan, my pump now delays turning on, then when it comes on it runs continuously until it has drained the pan and stops without restarting several times. It is much less annoying and less wear on the pump.

There are many other options for a shower. My solution was inexpensive and met my needs, however it is not the only option.

Get a portable toilet! You can often find these on craigslist.org which are damaged or no longer needed. Cut out the seat area if it's still there and you instantly have a building that would work as a shower. A benefit of this approach is it does not look like a shower to anyone who comes into your building. It may even already have a drain in the bottom. These can be expensive, around $300 used, but all you need to turn them into a shower is a water connection, an all-in-one shower head/valve and drain. Search craigslist.org for keywords *portable toilet* and *portable bathroom*, *portajohn*, or *porta potty*. If you need to put your shower in your warehouse area, this is an easy way to have an instant enclosed shower.

You can also use camping showers with light-duty frames and privacy covers. These are not very strong and I am not sure how long they would last. These are sold as privacy shelter tents for the beach or pool. There are inflatable showers for swimming pools. You can find inflatable bathtubs for those times when you want a bath but do not want a bathtub around all the time.

I made my shower look like a shower but this is not necessary. You can build a shower like mine and then cover the outside with concrete board which is similar to dry wall but stands up to moisture. Then place a cardboard refrigerator box or in plywood around it to make it look like a big crate. Leave the top open for moisture to escape and you have a shower that can be placed in a raw warehouse space. It even looks like it should be there. No one would think it was a shower and it does not have to be in the bathroom. You can build one like mine, then tape black plastic sheeting around the outside so it does not look like a shower but like a wrapped crate that has not been unpacked. There are many ways to camouflage a shower.

Some warehouses have no plumbing or bathrooms, but those are the cheapest ones too. If you have an RV and are accustomed to the RV lifestyle, you may want to park your RV in the warehouse, eat and sleep in it, and then you have the entire warehouse to work and play.

You will need to have your utilities set up. You want to set them up for a new account and not transfer them. You cannot transfer residential electricity to a commercial space. While you still have residential electricity, call your electric company to have the electricity service established for

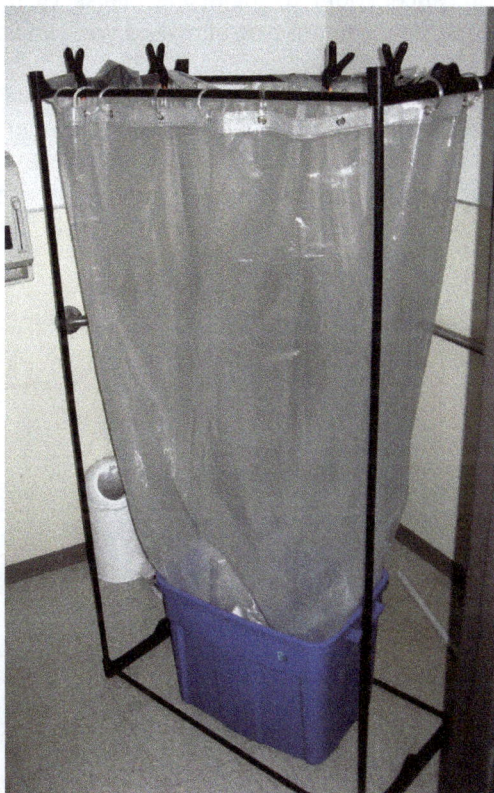

TOP: My temporary shower made from old shower curtains, a tub and a dog washer hose.
RIGHT TOP: Shower under construction.
RIGHT BOTTOM: Completed safety shower.

83

your commercial space. Do the same for the water if it is not included.

When you call to set up electric service they usually set up a business account which is separate from residential. They will ask if you want to use your federal tax ID number or your social security number. As a sole proprietorship, you do not have to use a tax ID number and can use your social security number. If you have a business tax number you can use that. Expect to pay a deposit that may be around $200 and a connection fee around $50. These will vary by location. Have a business name ready and you can use your own phone number. Have your PMB mailing address ready for bills and the physical address ready so they know where to set up service. Once you have your new service set up you can cancel your existing residential service. They will not ask a lot of questions about why you are canceling and you can say you are moving.

Transferring a regular phone is not difficult. There should be no issues with transferring your residential phone number to a commercial location. You may be subject to commercial rates, but these are not usually high for a single line. You can also abandon your landline and use your cell or a VOIP phone service because neither of those care where you live.

ABOVE: My shower during construction.
RIGHT: My final shower with sump
pump drain.

Transferring Internet and cable TV may be more complicated. Internet and cable TV services charge more for commercial locations than residential. If you can request a transfer online, that may be the easiest way and the installer may come out and set it up without asking any questions.

When I transferred my FIOS Internet and TV to my commercial warehouse the installer asked if I was living in the space. He knew I was moving from residential to commercial so I had to say yes. He asked if it was legal so I explained how there is an exception for living in an industrial or commercial area for artists and pointed out that such a place existed nearby where artists do live in a small upstairs and have a large work area in the bottom where they not only work but have weekly tours. I also had to say I was living here because if I did not, then he might have reported back that it was non-residential which would mean my rates would change. I never said I had the live-work exemption, only that it existed. Be prepared to answer questions if asked when you transfer your phone, TV or Internet. The good thing is that I was allowed to keep my existing package by transferring and did not have to pay the higher commercial rate. I did have some problems scheduling the installation. The computer system kicked out my installation three times because it identified the transfer as residential to commercial and could not process that. It took three calls before a supervisor approved it manually and a tech actually showed up, so be prepared for questions or problems and remember the magic phrase, "live-work space." Even if you do have to pay the commercial rate, if you picked the location carefully you should still be saving a lot of money each month.

Your car insurance company wants to know where your car is garaged. You can tell them you store your car at your office because it can be locked up there and live with your girl/boyfriend who is only a couple of miles away. This way you do not have to give a physical home address. Telling them you are living a couple of miles away also resolves issues about how far you drive to work which affects your insurance rate. Since you live where you work you do not have to drive which means you are also not driving every day.

Another consideration is watching movies or TV in the daytime. If you are in a single office only space surrounded by other offices with thin walls then your neighbors will hear every movie and be very annoyed. You may have to use headphones during the day to watch TV or listen to music. A warehouse/multi-office space is usually larger and may even have concrete walls between spaces which keeps the noise level down. This is another reason I prefer combination warehouse/office spaces.

Concrete floors are not appealing. Your office area should have carpet. You may want to extend your living area into the concrete warehouse. Cover concrete or commercial tile floors with rugs for a nice look and feel. You can find cheap rugs on craigslist.org or at your home supply store. Garage sales are also good places to look for rugs people no longer need. Some good keywords are *Persian rug runner, oriental rug* and *hall rug* or *carpet*. Some people do not know the difference between carpet and a rug. They will post nice rugs using the wrong terms so check both words.

Buy air purifiers rated to clean a space larger than your office area or have one in each office area rated for more than that area. You are in an industrial zone so there will always be more dust and pollutants in the air. This pollution comes not just from manufacturing but also from the fact that you are in an area with a lot of vehicle traffic during the day. This stirs up dirt and produces pollution.

A washer and dryer are also important. You can use the local laundromat, but that is a hassle.

Your washer needs hot and cold water plus 120V power and a drain. If you can place it close to your bathroom or kitchenette or in your kitchenette then this may be an easy installation. If you need to place it a distance away from a drain, you may need another sump pump to drain away the water. The dryer will require 220V AC power and an exhaust port. This will have to already be installed or you will have to hire an electrician to install it, which can be expensive. There are 120V small washers, but they are inefficient and can take a long time to dry clothes. Do not exhaust the dryer into your living space. It will pump in high humidity air and small particles that you do not want to breathe. Only run the exhaust outside. There are devices that are supposed to let you vent indoors, but those have a lot of back pressure and are not efficient. I used the old clothesline method in my warehouse for a long time. I would hang clothes on a temporary line and let an oscillating fan blow on them. This took overnight to dry clothes. A washer and dryer can indicate a residential space. You will want to place a rollaway shelf or some other large item in front of them when they are not in use to keep your space from looking too lived-in.

Living in a commercial space may limit your ability to vote. Voting regulations require you to provide a residential address. If you provide a mailbox service, PO box or commercial address, they will cross check and reject the address. You will receive a notice in the mail saying you need to resubmit your application with a residential address. If you have no residential address, you may not be able to register to vote. You do have the option to use a commercial address as your mailing address, which gives the option of using a friend or family or random address close to your actual address and using your commercial address or PMB as your mailing address.

You may be tempted to put a "closed" sign on the door to keep everyone out. A closed sign says the place is empty, which may make it attractive for burglars. It is better to keep them unsure whether someone is working there or not. Black out the door if it is a glass door and use a light timer to turn visible lights on at night.

Look for opportunities to monetize your space. Do you have a visually appealing space with aged red brick that photographers want to rent? Do you have a space that can be used as a data center with a corner where you can rent out equipment rack space? Are you willing to rent out some warehouse space to a small business or rent indoor parking for a trailer or mobile home? If you live in a school or church, you can rent out classrooms to artists or rent a gym or theatre for events. Renting spaces like this to the public requires insurance, permits and extra maintenance. You may want to split your front retail space or warehouse space into cubicles that you can rent to start-up companies or start an incubator business that provides office and phone service for fledgling companies.

This will take up some of your wonderful space but may help pay the rent too.

Maintaining the Illusion

You want your space to appear as commercial as possible from the outside and inside. You will likely meet clients if you are running your own business or you will eventually meet with the landlord or some representative of the landlord in your space. Your neighbors will see you come and go and see into your space when you open the roll-up door to pull your car out. This is why it is important to look as commercial as you can.

If you work a regular job and leave for work every morning at the same time it will look fishy to your neighbors. You can always say you work at night and are going home to sleep if they ask. You can also leave early before your neighbors start to arrive.

Having friends over to party every night can attract negative attention, too. However, if you play in a band, all you have to say is you work during the day and your band practices in your warehouse at night. Nothing wrong with that.

Do not expect to have a Thanksgiving get-together at your space or any family get-together at all. With the money you save on monthly rent, you can rent a party space at a local party hosting business if you need to host family events.

The 16 ft ceilings really make a space bigger than you think. Most of us are used to an apartment or house where you have one level. In a warehouse, you can build up and use it for storage. If you really wanted to go crazy, you could build out the warehouse into a two-story mini home, live in the top area and still have a lot of headroom on the working first floor. This would require some significant expense and building skills.

If your landlord asks for an emergency contact form to be filled out, you do not want to leave the home phone blank or use the same number for your home and office. Make sure you have cell, home and office phone numbers. You can set up a free phone number at Google voice but you must use your Google voice number regularly; otherwise, it will be automatically canceled. You can also use a VOIP service for a second phone line.

Keep everything in cabinets or drawers where it is not seen. This makes the place look organized and clean, but it also hides personal grooming items and personal property. You do not want a hair dryer lying out in the bathroom so put a cabinet in the bathroom to hold your dryer and other morning ritual products. Once it is closed, it looks like a generic storage cabinet. Cheap cabinets are always available on craigslist.org, which is where I bought most of my furniture.

Obviously, if you are walking around in your reception office in your boxer shorts at 9 AM and your neighbors can see you through the glass, it is harder to explain. Use some common sense. Cover the doors and windows so you can keep your space private. White sheeting is available from home supply stores and can be placed over windows. It allows natural light to come in but acts like frosted glass so no one can see activity inside. Black sheeting is also available if you want to completely block light and this plastic is very inexpensive. A glass front door can be blacked out using black foam core sheets from the office supply store. Cut and tape it in place. It looks like the office is empty and dark. I have had many people walk up and cup their hand over their eyes as they press their face to the glass to see if anyone was home without realizing the glass was blacked out.

In my complex there is another unit where three guys live. Everyone knows they live there because their personal cars are always parked outside. The neighbors do not know I live in my space because they cannot see my car. They do not see me for days at a time because I do not have to leave every day since I work and live in the same place. I may leave at noon to run errands when many neighbors are out for lunch and they only see me return at 2 or 3 pm. I may not go out until 7 PM and return at midnight when no one else is around. Even if the guys who live in the complex see me, they can never be sure if I am dropping my car off to store it in my space or coming in to work late or early.

Never leave anything outside your space. Nothing! Not even legitimate business equipment or supplies and certainly not pink flamingos, flower pots, tricycles or anything you might expect in front of a house.

Conclusion

You are now prepared to look for your alternative living space.

Every time I pull into my space I think of the flashy introduction to the Vega$ TV show and can see Robert Urich jump out of his car. I have space for art projects or just to relax. As I said at the beginning,

My only regret is that I did not do this years earlier.

I have touched on a handful of alternative living spaces. You may find even more specialized or unique spaces in your area. There is no end to what you can do with an alternative living space. You can be as creative as you want with your decor and spend as much or as little as you want. I have recommended craigslist.org and garage sales many times because they were my primary means of finding furniture and supplies at a fraction of the cost new furniture would cost.

Having so much extra space for storage and to work on art projects has made my life much easier. Giving up paying rent on a house also helps me save a lot of money each month.

Living in commercially or industrially zoned areas is not uncommon, but it is also not legal except in special circumstances. My advice is aimed at those who can find a space to live legally and keep a low profile. If you choose to be one of those who live life on the edge and live in non-residential settings successfully whether or not you get permission, good luck in your adventure.

If I have only made you think about the world and shown you that there are alternatives to what we are told by society, then it has been worthwhile.

Make a list of things you need to do next and start on the first item today.